Dot to Dot

How to solve a dot-to-dot puzzle

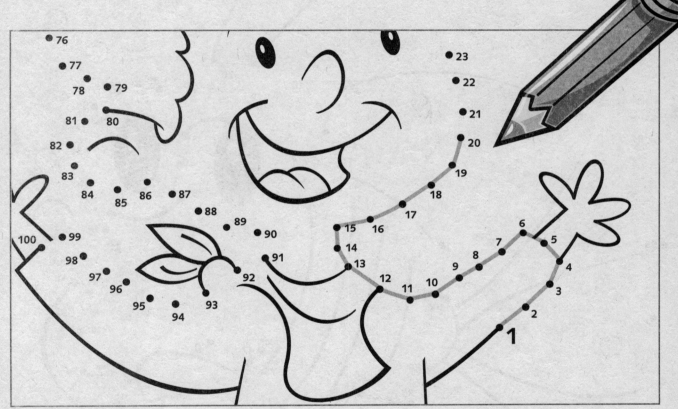

Each puzzle consists of a sequence of 100 numbered dots. The goal is to reveal a hidden picture by connecting each dot in order, starting with 1 and ending with 100.

Start by finding the number 1 and place your pencil on the dot next to it. Draw a line from the dot to the dot next to number 2. Then, without lifting your pencil, draw a line to the dot next to number 3. Continue connecting the dots in numerical order until you reach dot #100 to reveal the hidden picture.

When the puzzle is complete, you are ready to color the drawing you have created!

NUMBERS 1 TO 100

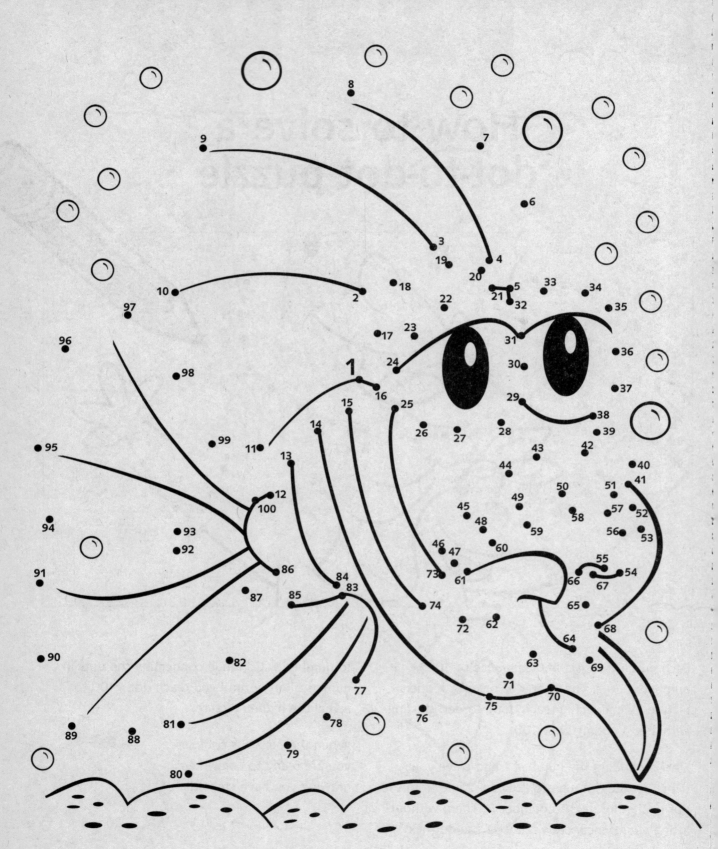

51 52 53 54 55 56 57 58 59 60 61 62 63 64 65 66 67 68 69 70 71 72 73 74 75
76 77 78 79 80 81 82 83 84 85 86 87 88 89 90 91 92 93 94 95 96 97 98 99 100

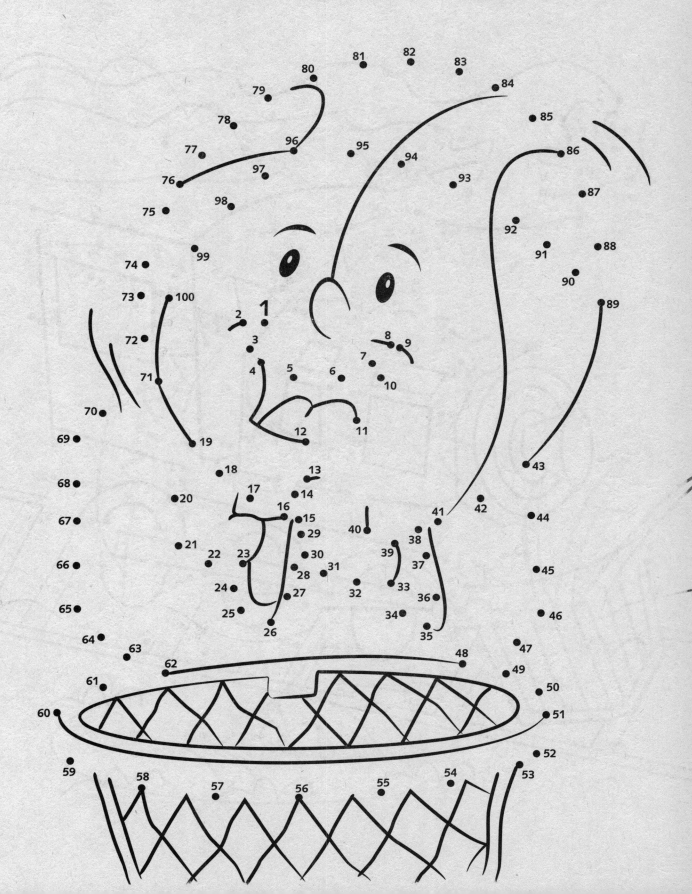

51 52 53 54 55 56 57 58 59 60 61 62 63 64 65 66 67 68 69 70 71 72 73 74 75
76 77 78 79 80 81 82 83 84 85 86 87 88 89 90 91 92 93 94 95 96 97 98 99 100

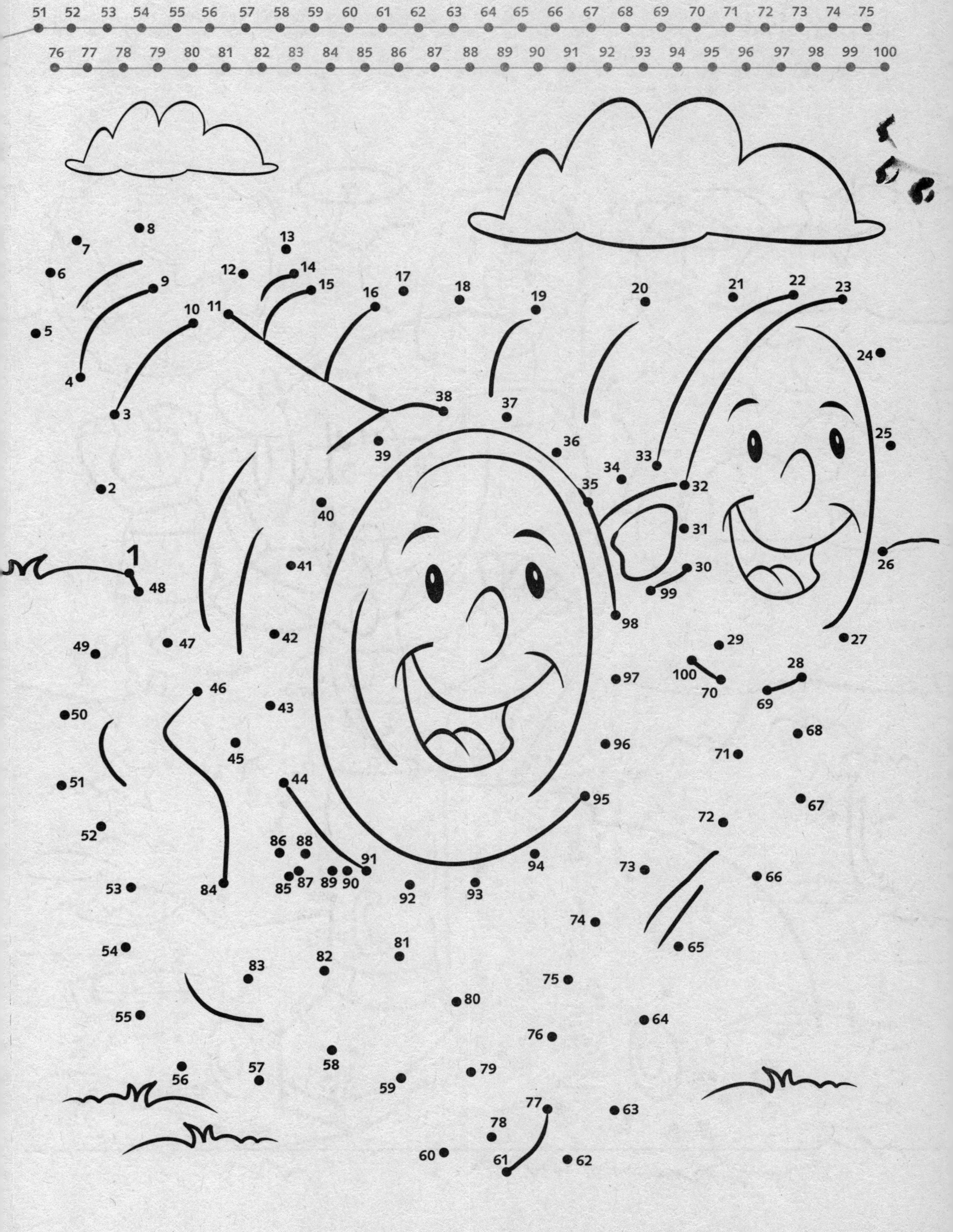

1 2 3 4 5 6 7 8 9 10 11 12 13 14 15 16 17 18 19 20 21 22 23 24 25
26 27 28 29 30 31 32 33 34 35 36 37 38 39 40 41 42 43 44 45 46 47 48 49 50

1 2 3 4 5 6 7 8 9 10 11 12 13 14 15 16 17 18 19 20 21 22 23 24 25
26 27 28 29 30 31 32 33 34 35 36 37 38 39 40 41 42 43 44 45 46 47 48 49 50

51 52 53 54 55 56 57 58 59 60 61 62 63 64 65 66 67 68 69 70 71 72 73 74 75

76 77 78 79 80 81 82 83 84 85 86 87 88 89 90 91 92 93 94 95 96 97 98 99 100

51 52 53 54 55 56 57 58 59 60 61 62 63 64 65 66 67 68 69 70 71 72 73 74 75
76 77 78 79 80 81 82 83 84 85 86 87 88 89 90 91 92 93 94 95 96 97 98 99 100

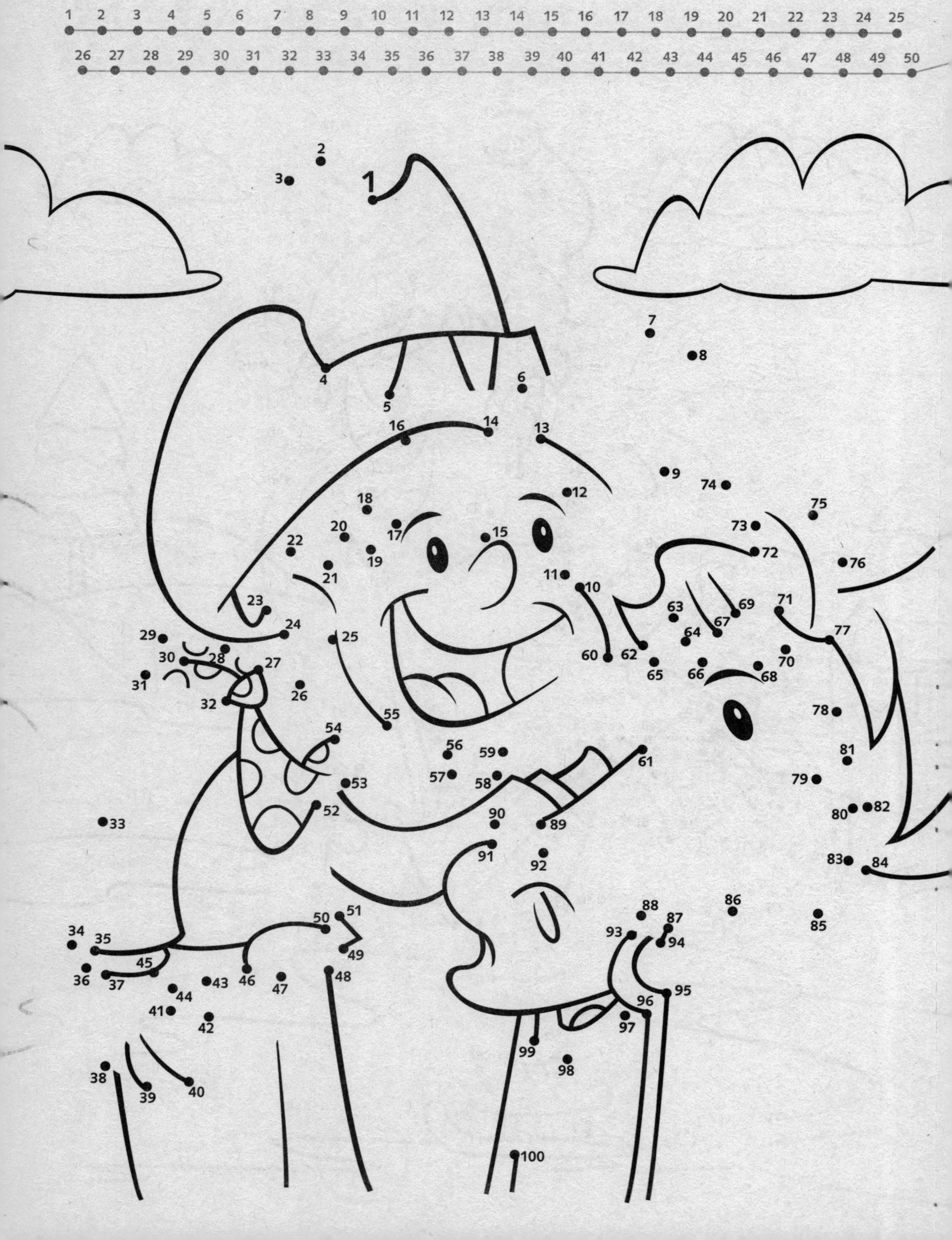

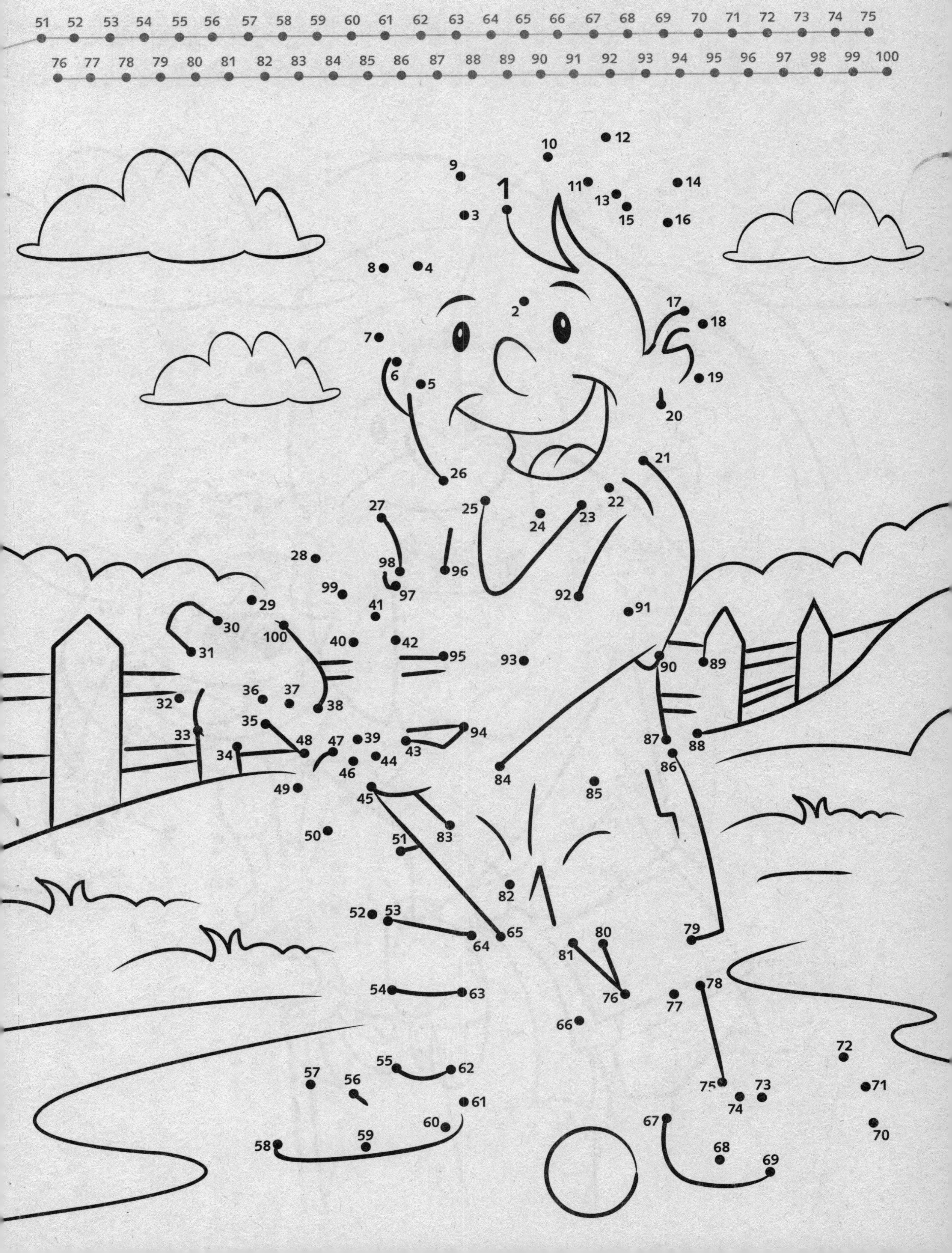

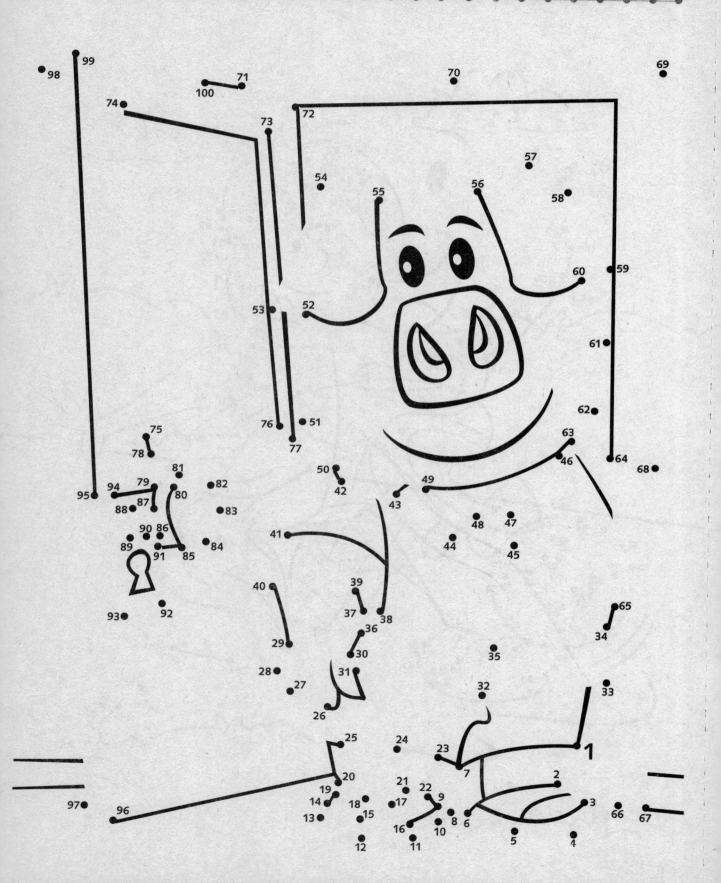

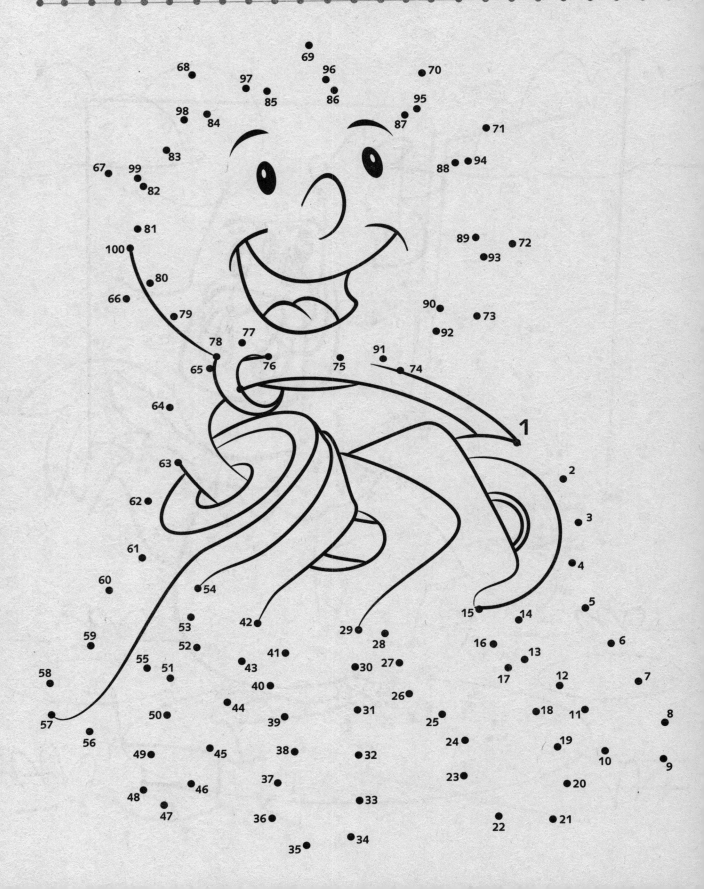

1 2 3 4 5 6 7 8 9 10 11 12 13 14 15 16 17 18 19 20 21 22 23 24 25
26 27 28 29 30 31 32 33 34 35 36 37 38 39 40 41 42 43 44 45 46 47 48 49 50

51 52 53 54 55 56 57 58 59 60 61 62 63 64 65 66 67 68 69 70 71 72 73 74 75

76 77 78 79 80 81 82 83 84 85 86 87 88 89 90 91 92 93 94 95 96 97 98 99 100

92 93 94 95

56 91
55 57 90 96
54 89 97
53 51 52 50 58 84 85 98
49 59 82 83 88 99
48 60 81 86 100
47 61 80 79 78 87 1
46 45 62 77 2
63 76 14 3
64 75 13 4
65 74 12 5
44 39 38 37 67 68 69 11 10 9
43 40 36 66 15 8 6 7
42 41 35 70 73 72 16 17
34 33 32 71 18
31 19
30 20
29 21
28 22
27 26 25 24 23

1 2 3 4 5 6 7 8 9 10 11 12 13 14 15 16 17 18 19 20 21 22 23 24 25
26 27 28 29 30 31 32 33 34 35 36 37 38 39 40 41 42 43 44 45 46 47 48 49 50

1 2 3 4 5 6 7 8 9 10 11 12 13 14 15 16 17 18 19 20 21 22 23 24 25

26 27 28 29 30 31 32 33 34 35 36 37 38 39 40 41 42 43 44 45 46 47 48 49 50

51 52 53 54 55 56 57 58 59 60 61 62 63 64 65 66 67 68 69 70 71 72 73 74 75

76 77 78 79 80 81 82 83 84 85 86 87 88 89 90 91 92 93 94 95 96 97 98 99 100

51 52 53 54 55 56 57 58 59 60 61 62 63 64 65 66 67 68 69 70 71 72 73 74 75

76 77 78 79 80 81 82 83 84 85 86 87 88 89 90 91 92 93 94 95 96 97 98 99 100

54 55
53 56
52 64
57 63 65
59 62 66
51 58 60 61 67
50 69 68 71
49 70 72
48 73 75
47 74 76
77
46 78
45 80 79
43 81
44 42 41 40 39 38 37 36 81
14 13 12 11
33 35 3 4 5 10
34 83 82
15
32 30 6 9
31 16 2 84 85
26 29 8 7 86
28 17 1 87
18 88
100
27 19 99
25 24 23 91
20 98 89
22 97 90
21 96 93 92
94
95

52

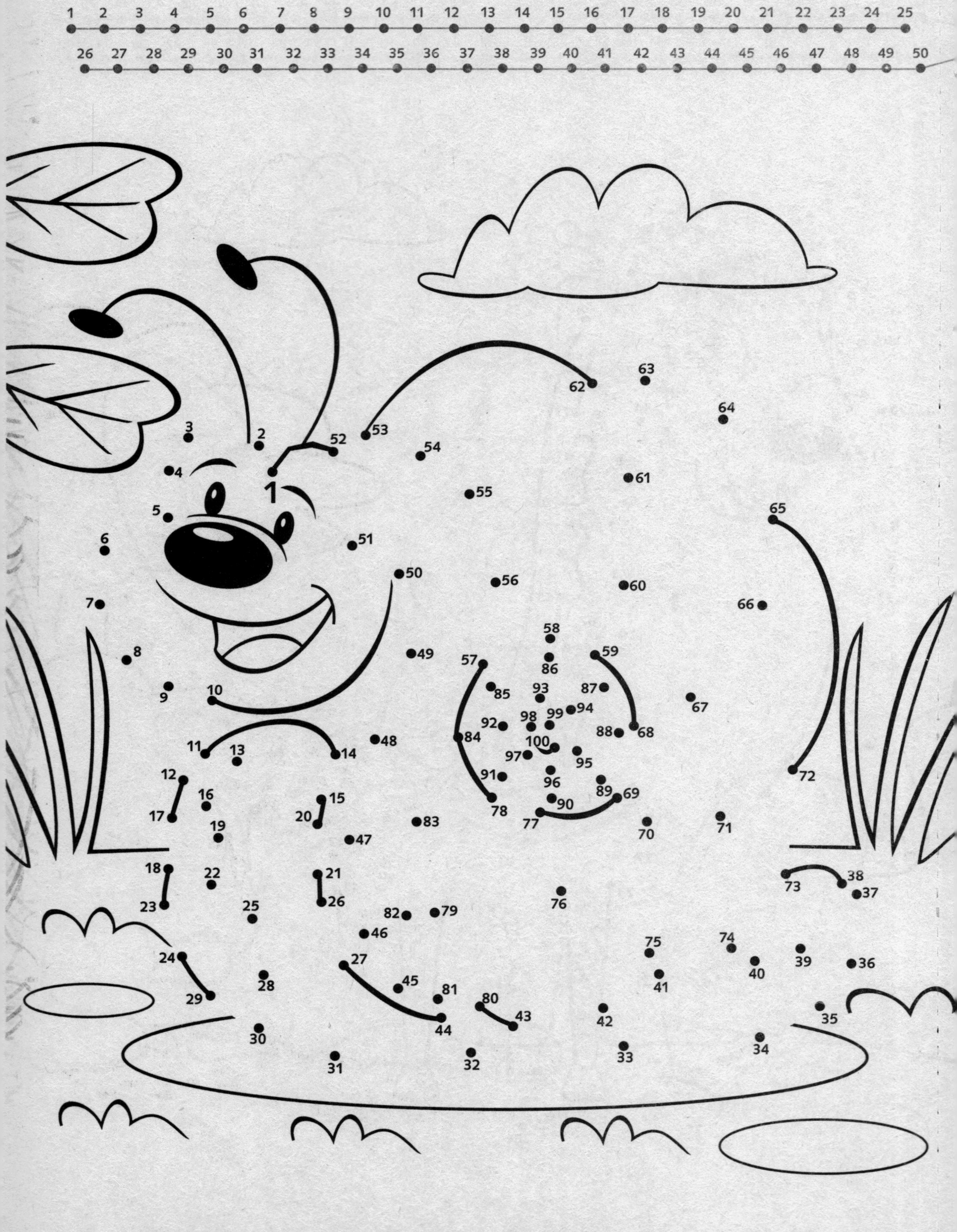

51 52 53 54 55 56 57 58 59 60 61 62 63 64 65 66 67 68 69 70 71 72 73 74 75
76 77 78 79 80 81 82 83 84 85 86 87 88 89 90 91 92 93 94 95 96 97 98 99 100

51 52 53 54 55 56 57 58 59 60 61 62 63 64 65 66 67 68 69 70 71 72 73 74 75
76 77 78 79 80 81 82 83 84 85 86 87 88 89 90 91 92 93 94 95 96 97 98 99 100

1 2 3 4 5 6 7 8 9 10 11 12 13 14 15 16 17 18 19 20 21 22 23 24 25
26 27 28 29 30 31 32 33 34 35 36 37 38 39 40 41 42 43 44 45 46 47 48 49 50

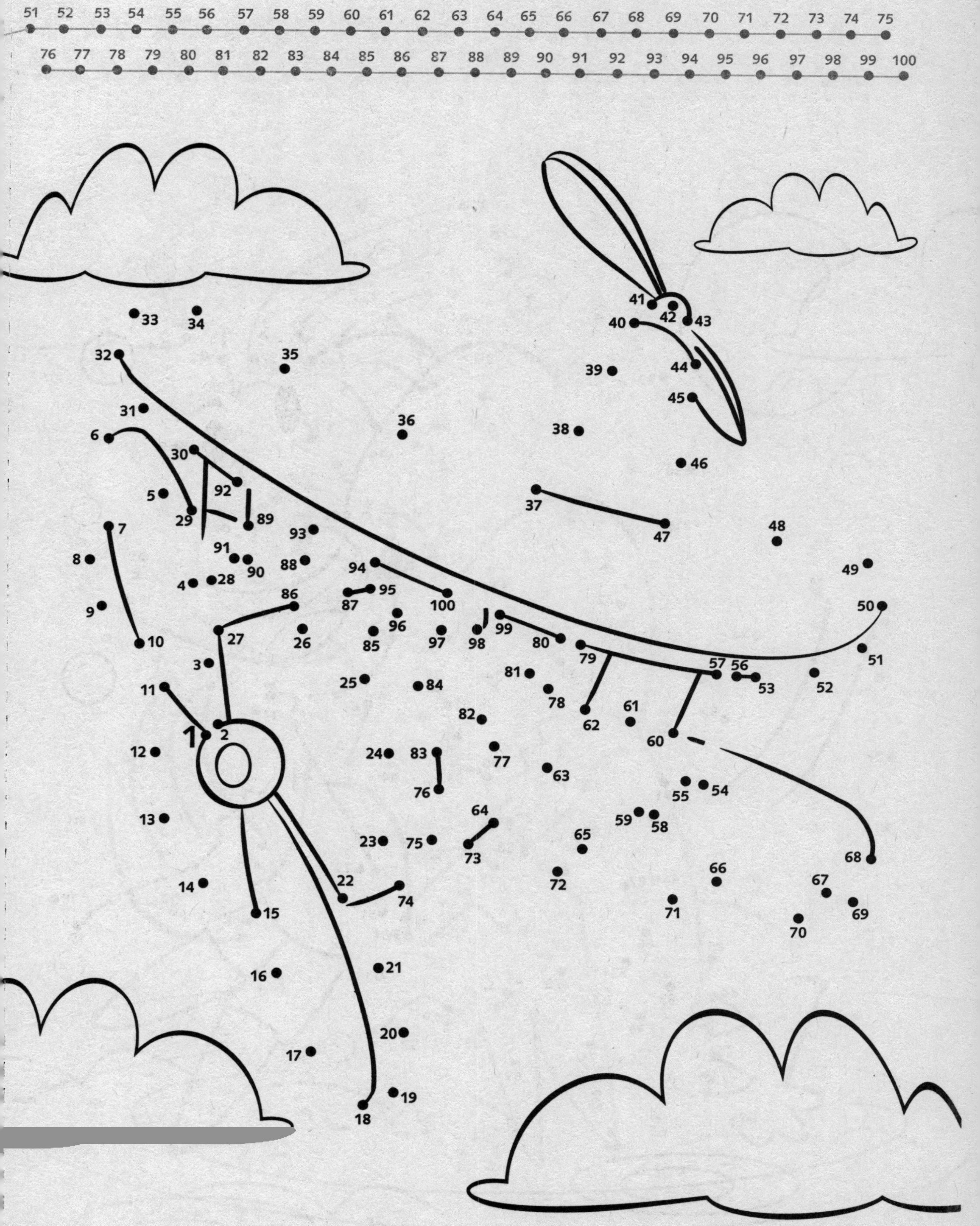

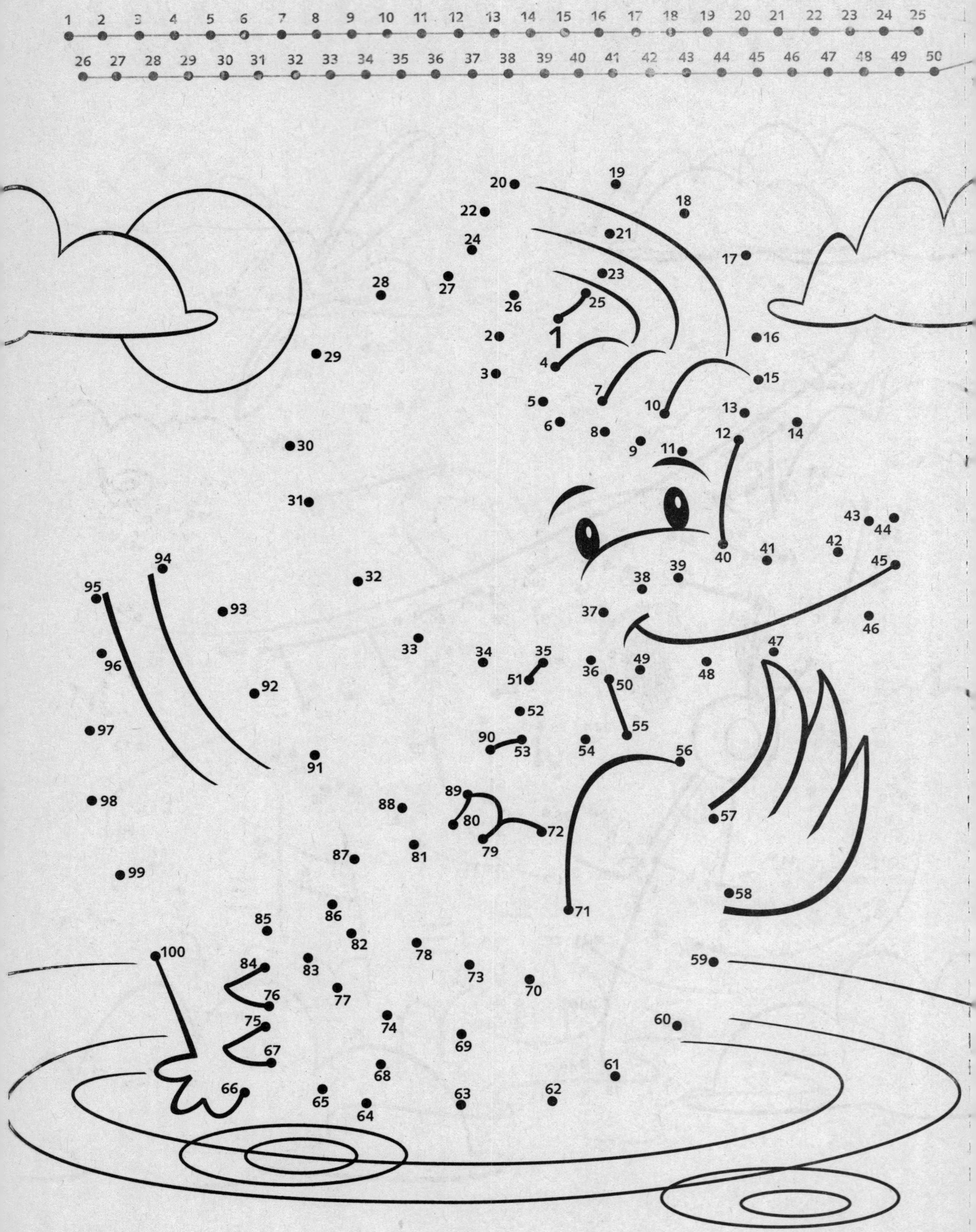
1 2 3 4 5 6 7 8 9 10 11 12 13 14 15 16 17 18 19 20 21 22 23 24 25
26 27 28 29 30 31 32 33 34 35 36 37 38 39 40 41 42 43 44 45 46 47 48 49 50

51 52 53 54 55 56 57 58 59 60 61 62 63 64 65 66 67 68 69 70 71 72 73 74 75
76 77 78 79 80 81 82 83 84 85 86 87 88 89 90 91 92 93 94 95 96 97 98 99 100

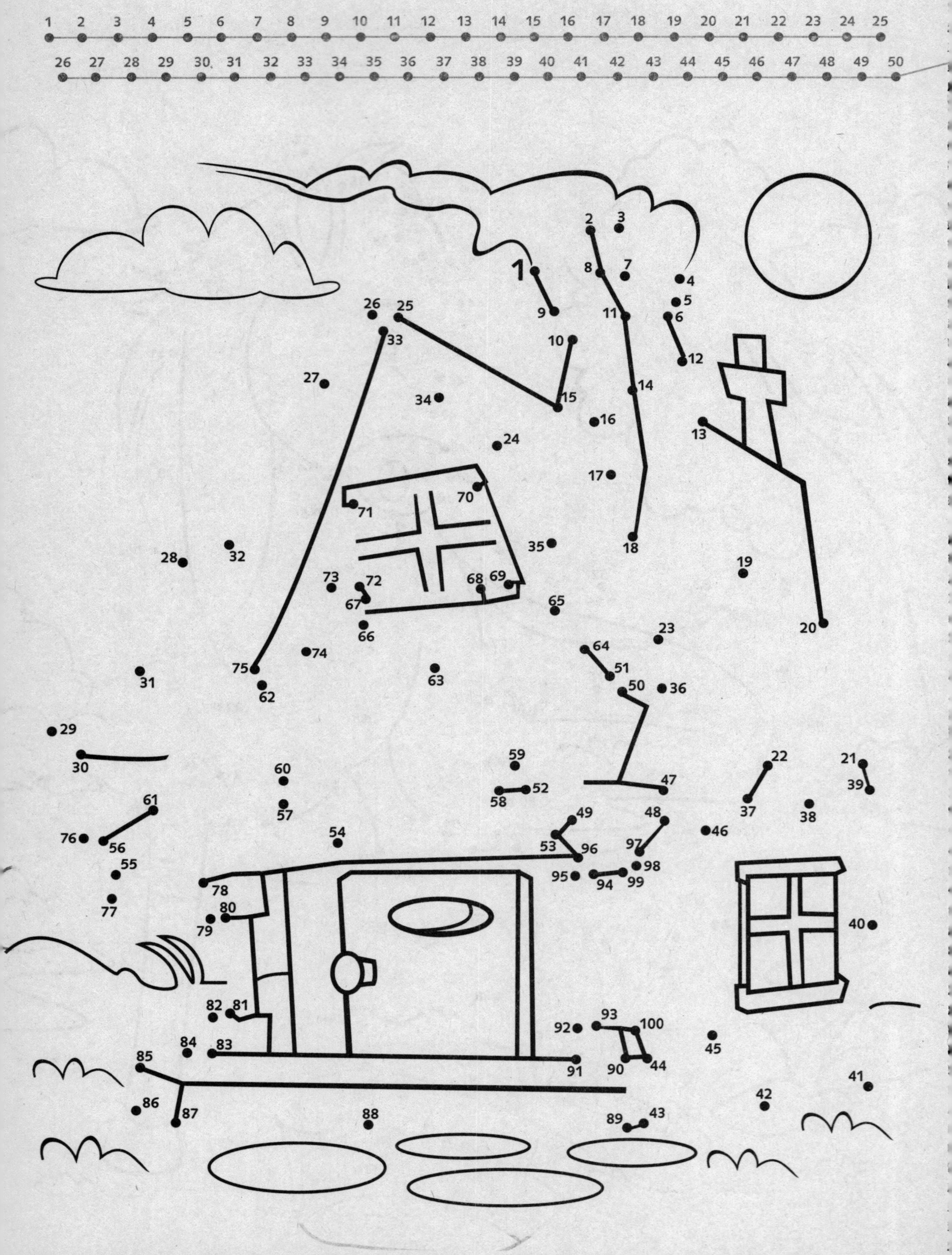

51 52 53 54 55 56 57 58 59 60 61 62 63 64 65 66 67 68 69 70 71 72 73 74 75
76 77 78 79 80 81 82 83 84 85 86 87 88 89 90 91 92 93 94 95 96 97 98 99 100

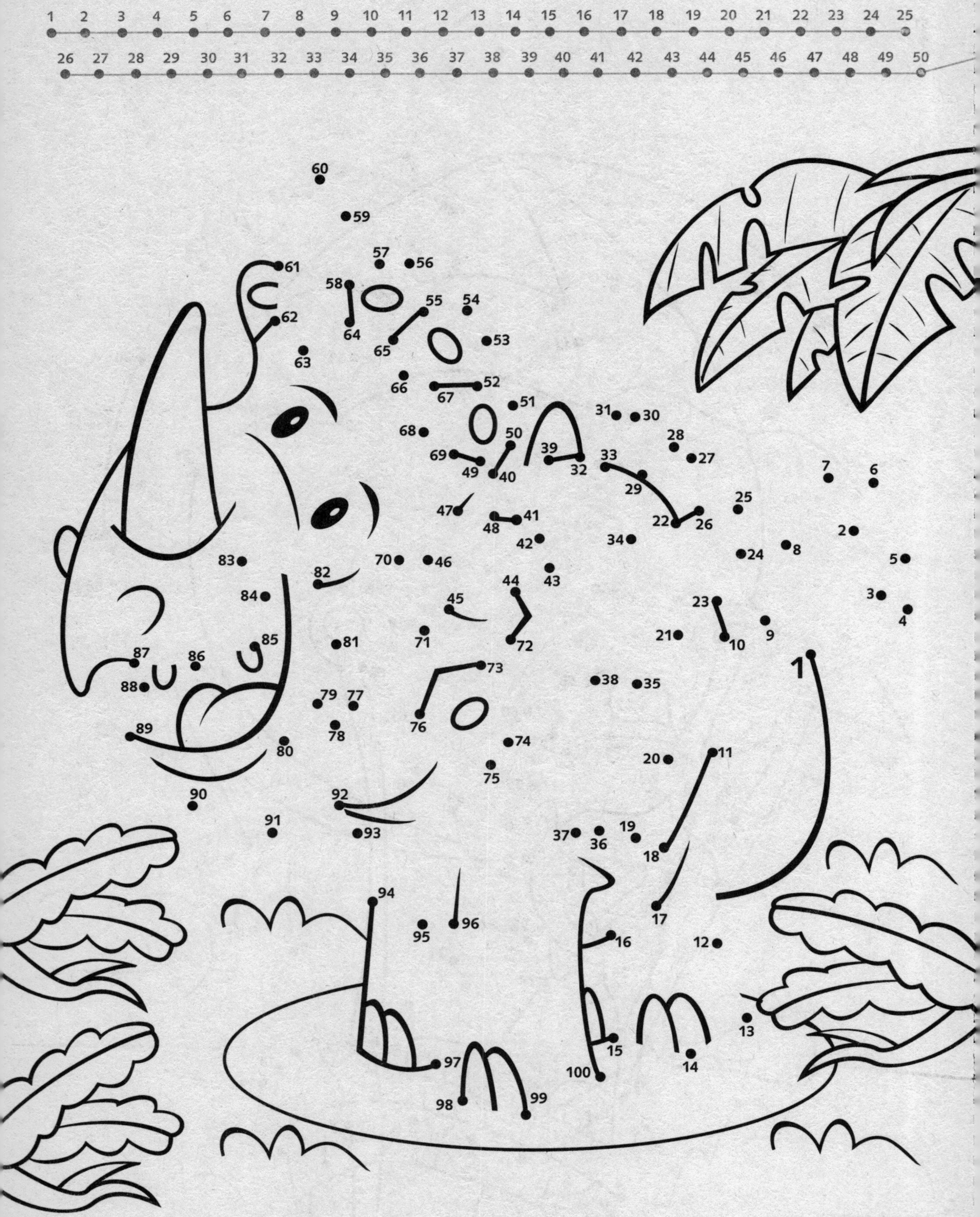

1 2 3 4 5 6 7 8 9 10 11 12 13 14 15 16 17 18 19 20 21 22 23 24 25
26 27 28 29 30 31 32 33 34 35 36 37 38 39 40 41 42 43 44 45 46 47 48 49 50

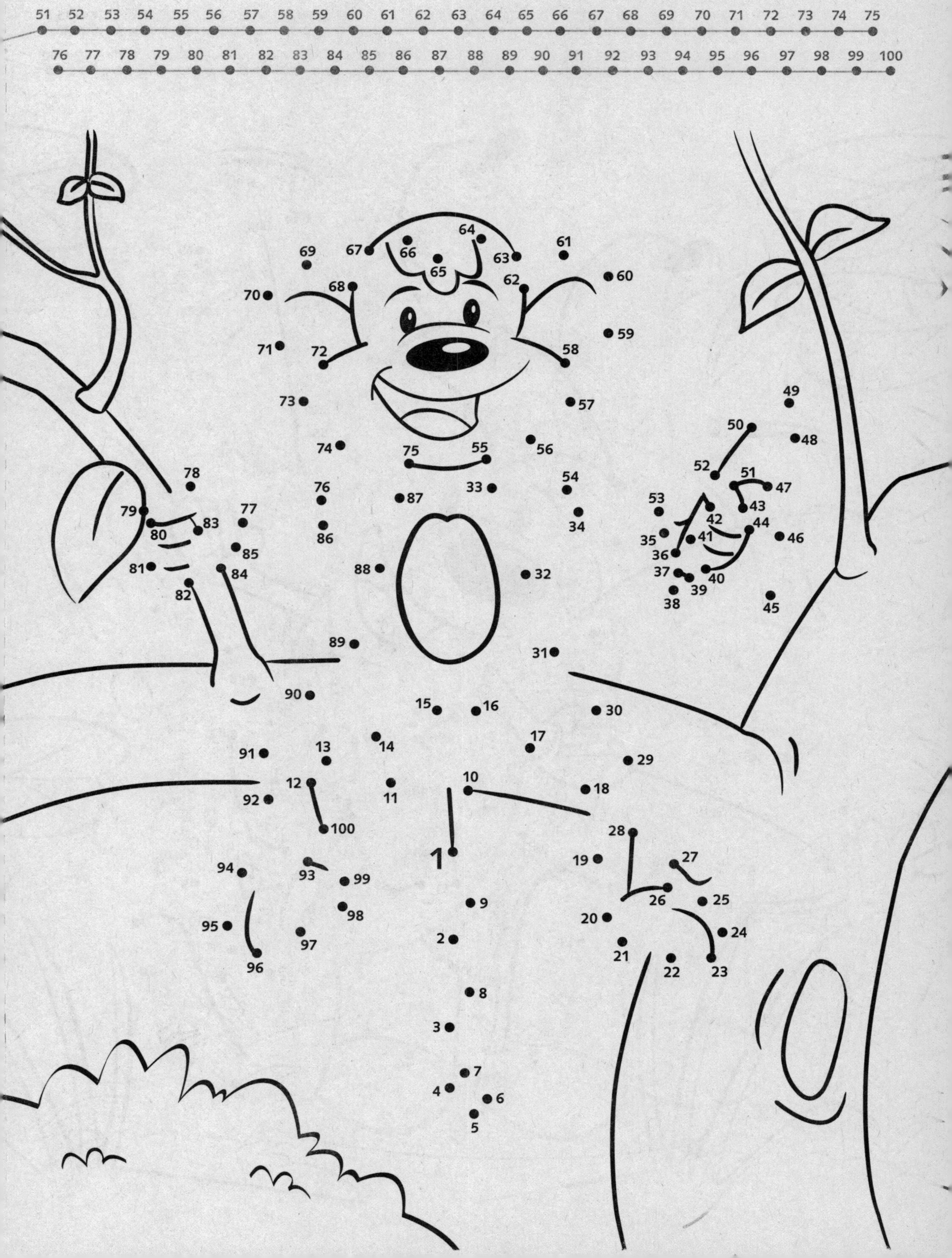

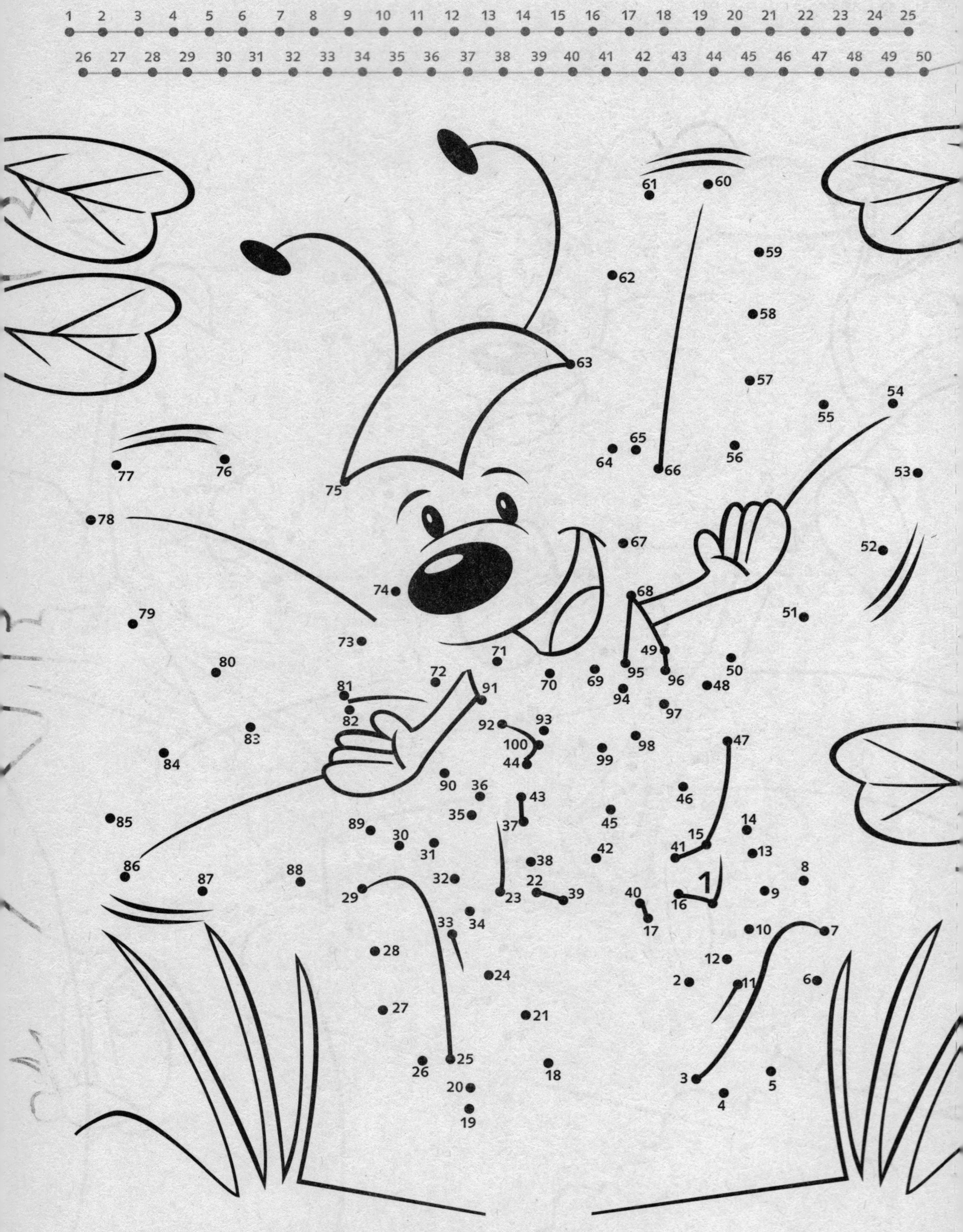

51 52 53 54 55 56 57 58 59 60 61 62 63 64 65 66 67 68 69 70 71 72 73 74 75
76 77 78 79 80 81 82 83 84 85 86 87 88 89 90 91 92 93 94 95 96 97 98 99 100

51 52 53 54 55 56 57 58 59 60 61 62 63 64 65 66 67 68 69 70 71 72 73 74 75
76 77 78 79 80 81 82 83 84 85 86 87 88 89 90 91 92 93 94 95 96 97 98 99 100

18 19
17 20
21 22
23
16
93 92
100
15 99 96
13 94 91
98
12 24
14 97 95 25
11 89 90 26
88 27
87
28
10 34
8 35 29
6 38 36 30
39
9 41 40 37 31
33 32
42
44
43
45
86 46
3 2 1 47 48
4 49
50
7 52
5 51
85 54 53
84 70 71
83 72 69 68 56
82 73 55
81 74 67 57
80 66 58
79 75 65 59
76 64 60
78 63 61
77 62

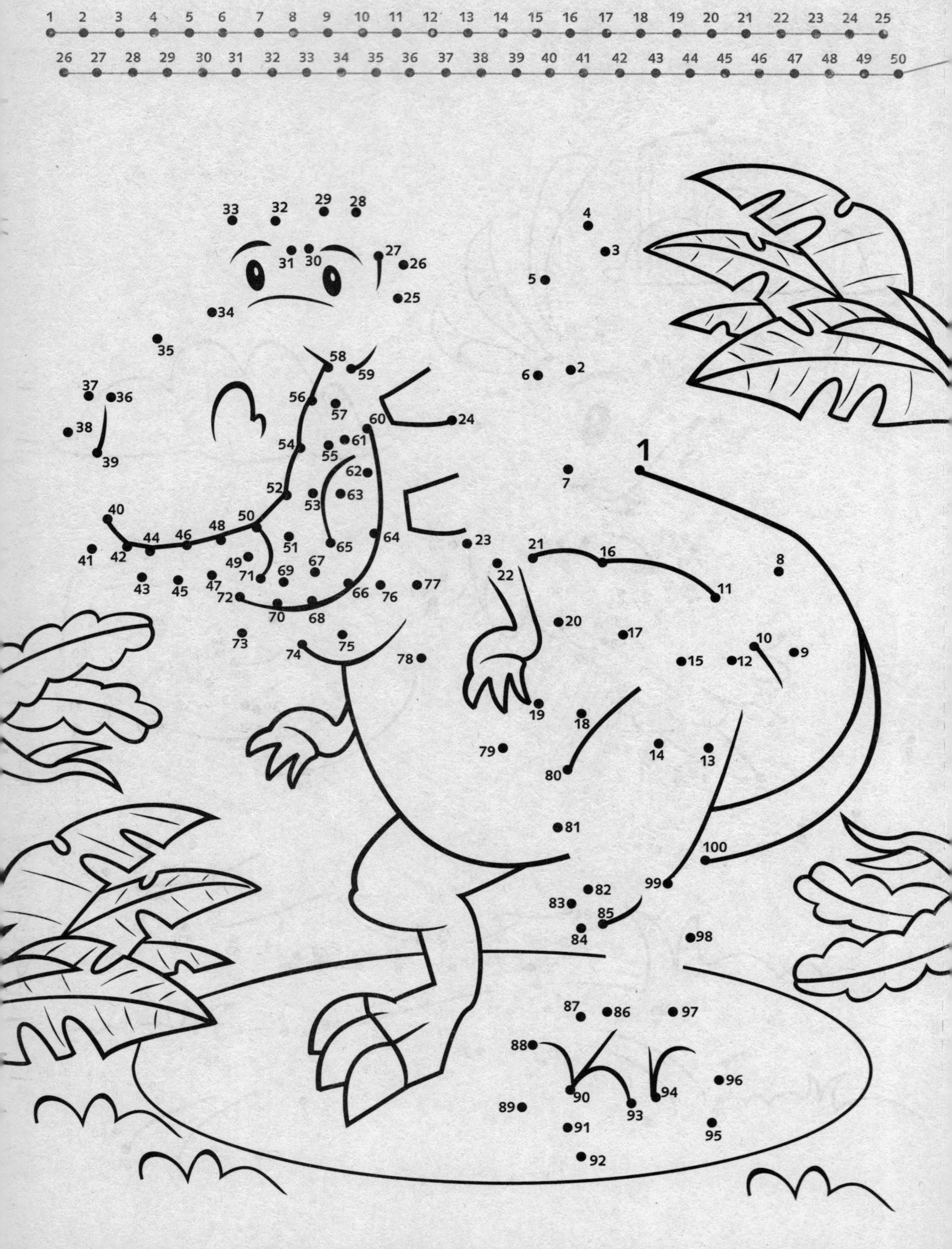

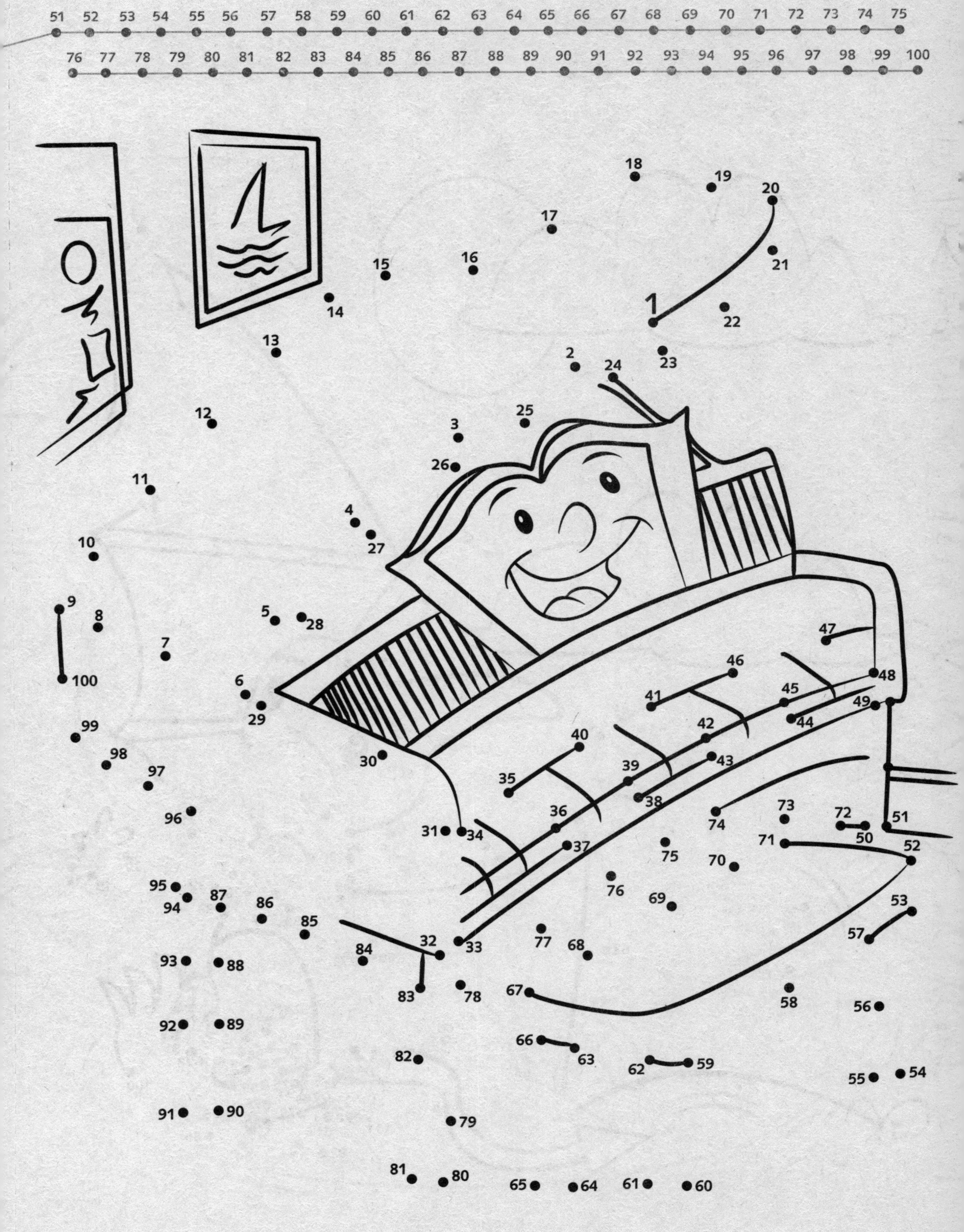

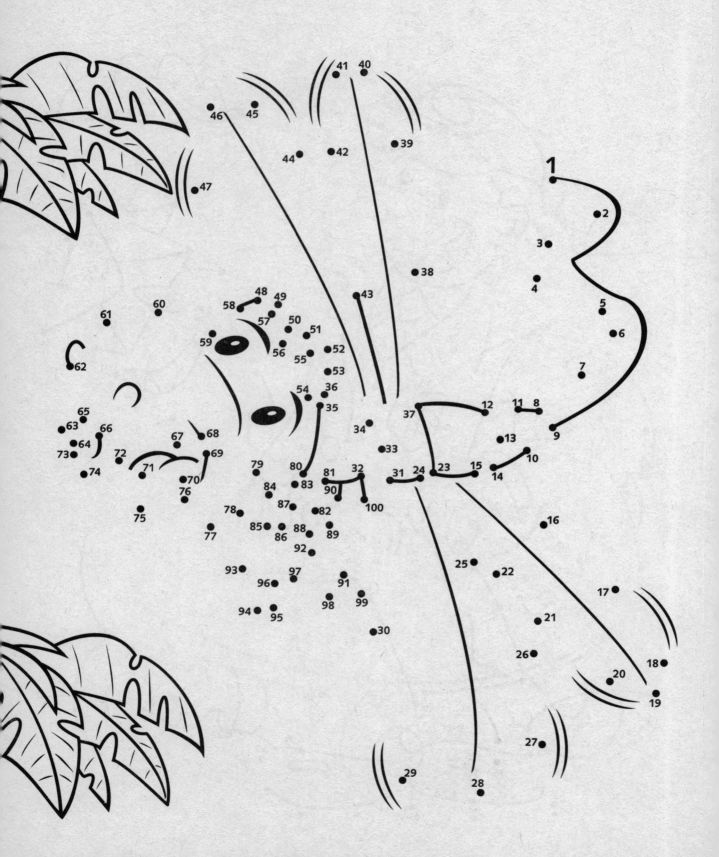

1 2 3 4 5 6 7 8 9 10 11 12 13 14 15 16 17 18 19 20 21 22 23 24 25
26 27 28 29 30 31 32 33 34 35 36 37 38 39 40 41 42 43 44 45 46 47 48 49 50

51 52 53 54 55 56 57 58 59 60 61 62 63 64 65 66 67 68 69 70 71 72 73 74 75

76 77 78 79 80 81 82 83 84 85 86 87 88 89 90 91 92 93 94 95 96 97 98 99 100

74 73 72
62 71
75 70
80 63
61 64 69
67
65 68
66
76 77 59 58
78 60 56
85 84 79 81 57
82 83 54 55
53 51 50
52
47 48 49
46 45 44
42 43
41
89 40 38
99 88 90 37
100 98 39 36
22 23 24 93
21 91 92 94 31
25 97 96 35 34 33 32 30
26 27 95 28 29
20
19 17
18 14
16 13 10
15 11 7
12 9 8 6 5 4
3 2
1

1 2 3 4 5 6 7 8 9 10 11 12 13 14 15 16 17 18 19 20 21 22 23 24 25

26 27 28 29 30 31 32 33 34 35 36 37 38 39 40 41 42 43 44 45 46 47 48 49 50

51 52 53 54 55 56 57 58 59 60 61 62 63 64 65 66 67 68 69 70 71 72 73 74 75

76 77 78 79 80 81 82 83 84 85 86 87 88 89 90 91 92 93 94 95 96 97 98 99 100

93 94 1 2 3
4 24
95 5 23 25
92 96 22 27
91 97 6 21 28 30 31 32 33
20 26 34
90 98 7 8 35 36
89 99 19 37 39 40
88 100 9 18 38 42 41
87 10 17 43
86 11 16 51 46 45 44
85 50 48 47
84 12 15 52 49
83 82 13 14 53 54 55 56 57
81 65 58
80 66 63 59
79 64 62 61 60
78 67
77 68
76 69
75 71 70
74 73 72

1 2 3 4 5 6 7 8 9 10 11 12 13 14 15 16 17 18 19 20 21 22 23 24 25
26 27 28 29 30 31 32 33 34 35 36 37 38 39 40 41 42 43 44 45 46 47 48 49 50

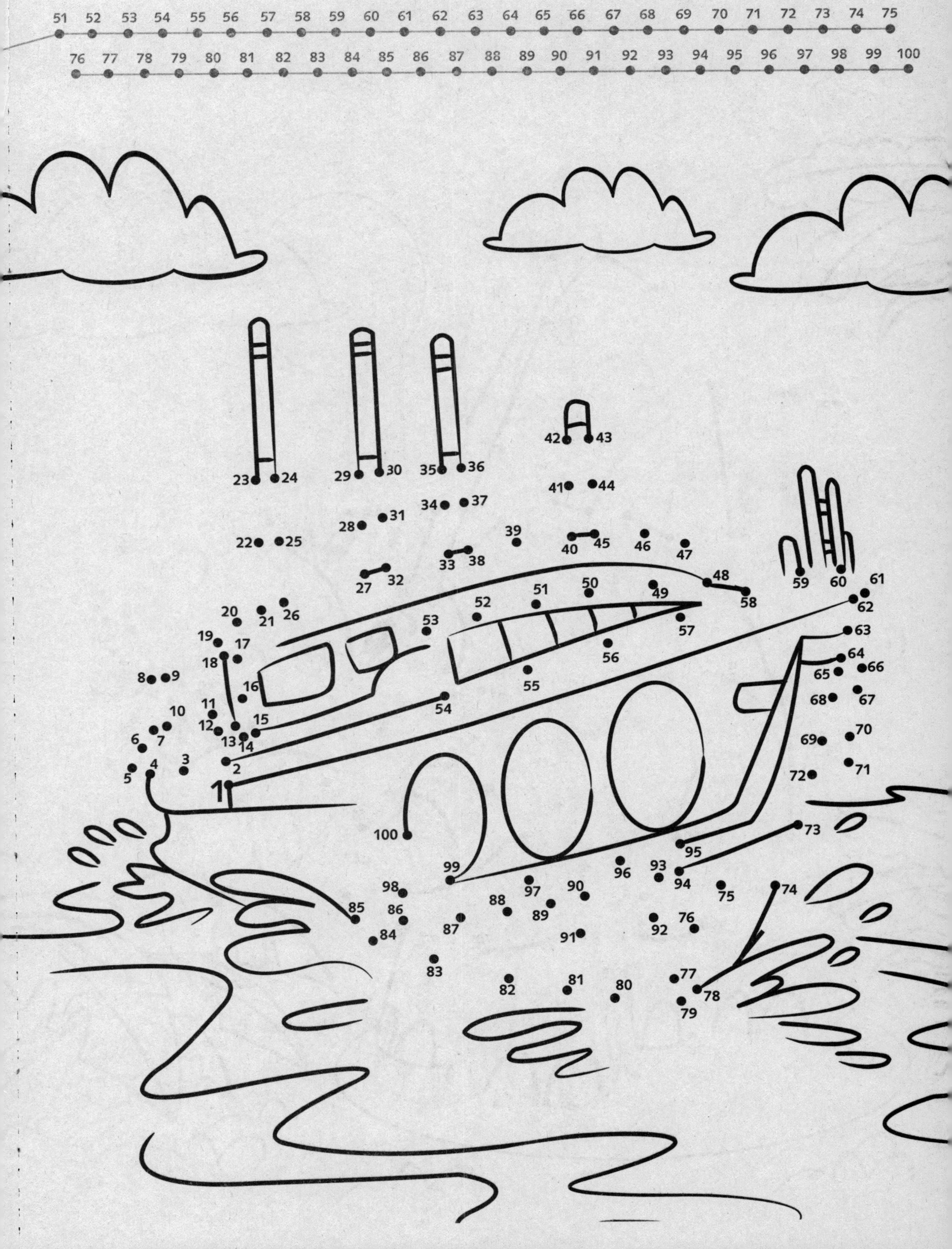

1 2 3 4 5 6 7 8 9 10 11 12 13 14 15 16 17 18 19 20 21 22 23 24 25
26 27 28 29 30 31 32 33 34 35 36 37 38 39 40 41 42 43 44 45 46 47 48 49 50

51 52 53 54 55 56 57 58 59 60 61 62 63 64 65 66 67 68 69 70 71 72 73 74 75
76 77 78 79 80 81 82 83 84 85 86 87 88 89 90 91 92 93 94 95 96 97 98 99 100

1 2 3 4 5 6 7 8 9 10 11 12 13 14 15 16 17 18 19 20 21 22 23 24 25
26 27 28 29 30 31 32 33 34 35 36 37 38 39 40 41 42 43 44 45 46 47 48 49 50

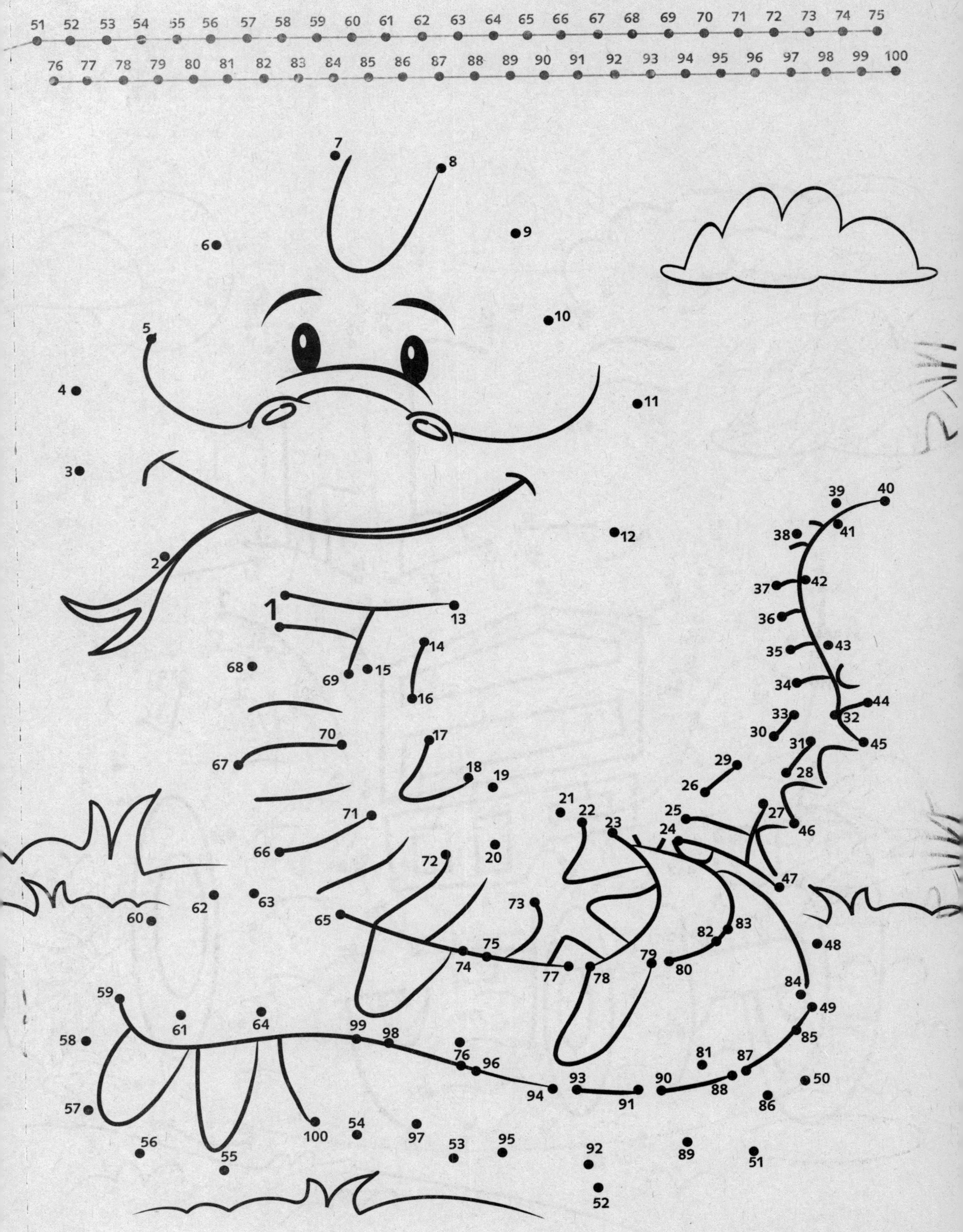

1 2 3 4 5 6 7 8 9 10 11 12 13 14 15 16 17 18 19 20 21 22 23 24 25

26 27 28 29 30 31 32 33 34 35 36 37 38 39 40 41 42 43 44 45 46 47 48 49 50

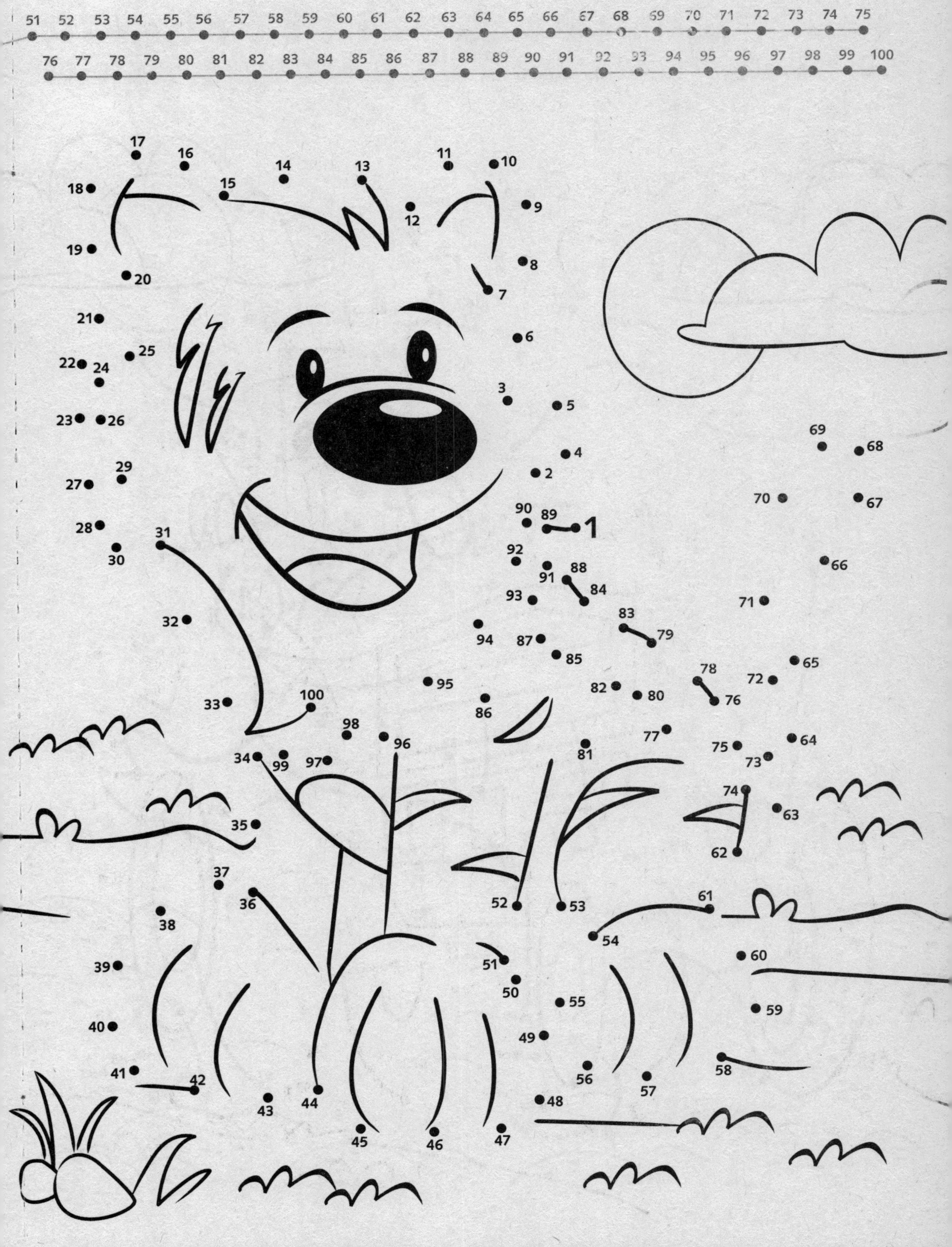

1 2 3 4 5 6 7 8 9 10 11 12 13 14 15 16 17 18 19 20 21 22 23 24 25
26 27 28 29 30 31 32 33 34 35 36 37 38 39 40 41 42 43 44 45 46 47 48 49 50

1 2 3 4 5 6 7 8 9 10 11 12 13 14 15 16 17 18 19 20 21 22 23 24 25

26 27 28 29 30 31 32 33 34 35 36 37 38 39 40 41 42 43 44 45 46 47 48 49 50

9 8
11
12 6
5
14 7
10 4 3
15 13
17 18
16 2
1
19
20
21
22
23 32 33
31 34
30 35
60 29 36
63 26 27 40
59 58 28 37
67 66 61 38
65 62 44 43 39
64
68 45
57 41
69 25
24 55
70 56 42
53
73 54 48
74 79 52 51
85 49 46
71 84 86 87 50
78 47
83
88
80
72 75 77 89
82 90 91
76 81 100
93 92
99 98
94 96 97
95

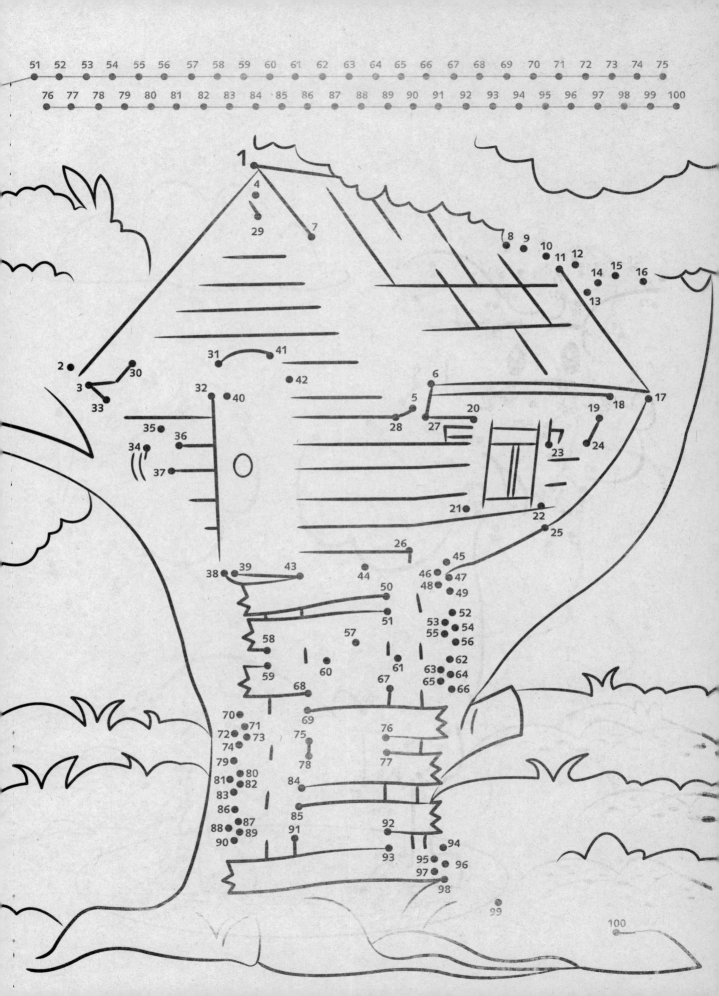

51 52 53 54 55 56 57 58 59 60 61 62 63 64 65 66 67 68 69 70 71 72 73 74 75
76 77 78 79 80 81 82 83 84 85 86 87 88 89 90 91 92 93 94 95 96 97 98 99 100

1 2 3 4 5 6 7 8 9 10 11 12 13 14 15 16 17 18 19 20 21 22 23 24 25
26 27 28 29 30 31 32 33 34 35 36 37 38 39 40 41 42 43 44 45 46 47 48 49 50

51 52 53 54 55 56 57 58 59 60 61 62 63 64 65 66 67 68 69 70 71 72 73 74 75
76 77 78 79 80 81 82 83 84 85 86 87 88 89 90 91 92 93 94 95 96 97 98 99 100

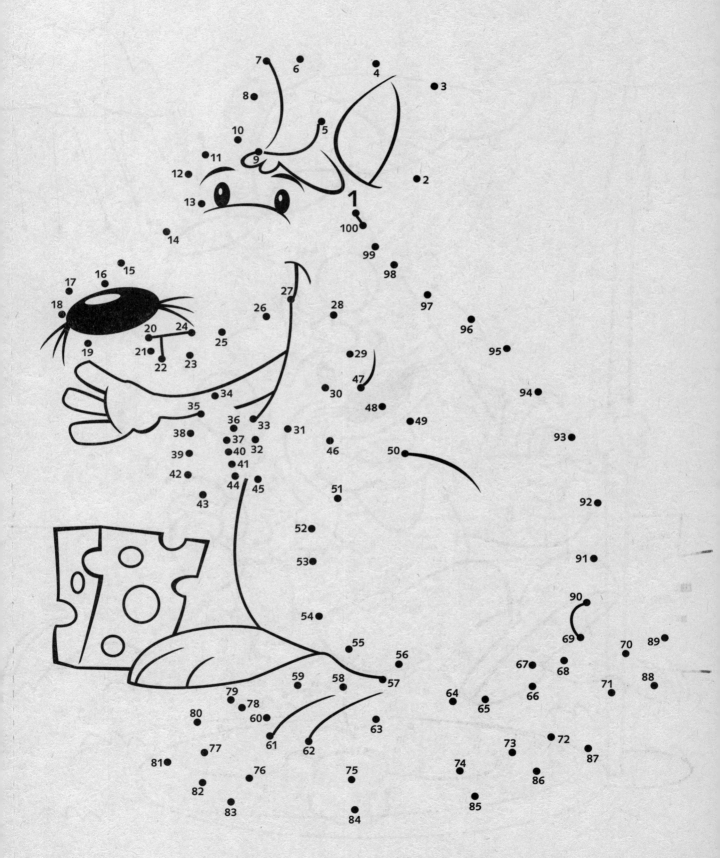

1 2 3 4 5 6 7 8 9 10 11 12 13 14 15 16 17 18 19 20 21 22 23 24 25
26 27 28 29 30 31 32 33 34 35 36 37 38 39 40 41 42 43 44 45 46 47 48 49 50

51 52 53 54 55 56 57 58 59 60 61 62 63 64 65 66 67 68 69 70 71 72 73 74 75
76 77 78 79 80 81 82 83 84 85 86 87 88 89 90 91 92 93 94 95 96 97 98 99 100

51 52 53 54 55 56 57 58 59 60 61 62 63 64 65 66 67 68 69 70 71 72 73 74 75

76 77 78 79 80 81 82 83 84 85 86 87 88 89 90 91 92 93 94 95 96 97 98 99 100

42 41 40
43
35
34
36 33
38 37
44 39
32
45
46
47 49
48
31
50
30
51
29
52
28 26
27 25
53 24
23
54 22
21
55 59
16
56 17 15 9 8
57 18 10
66 14 100 99 5 7
65 64 6
68 62 63 13 12 11 98
67 69 70 4
71 61 60 20 97
72
3
73 86 92 96 2
76 79 83 87 91 95
78 90 93
74 75 77 80 81 82 84 85 88 89 94
1

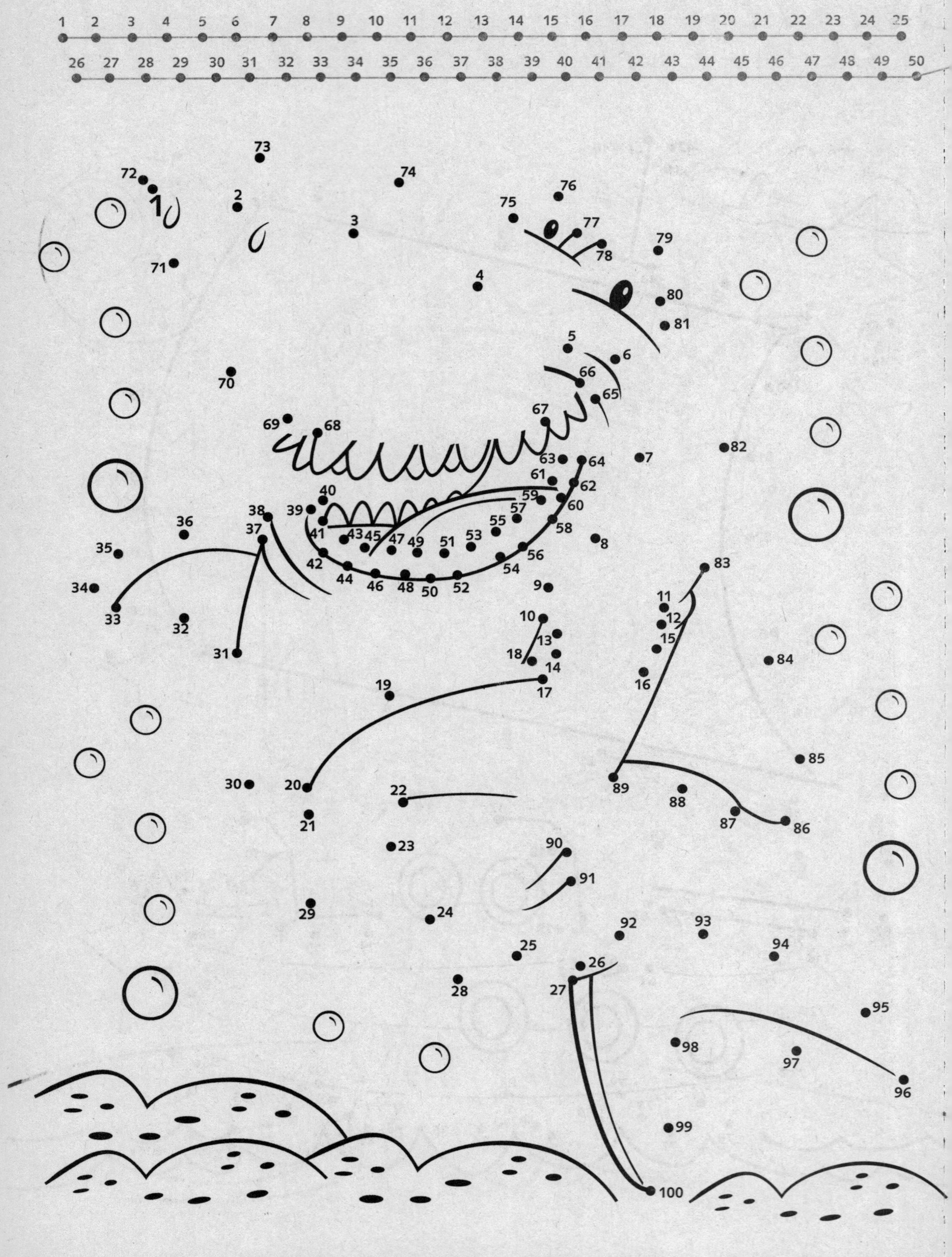
1 2 3 4 5 6 7 8 9 10 11 12 13 14 15 16 17 18 19 20 21 22 23 24 25
26 27 28 29 30 31 32 33 34 35 36 37 38 39 40 41 42 43 44 45 46 47 48 49 50

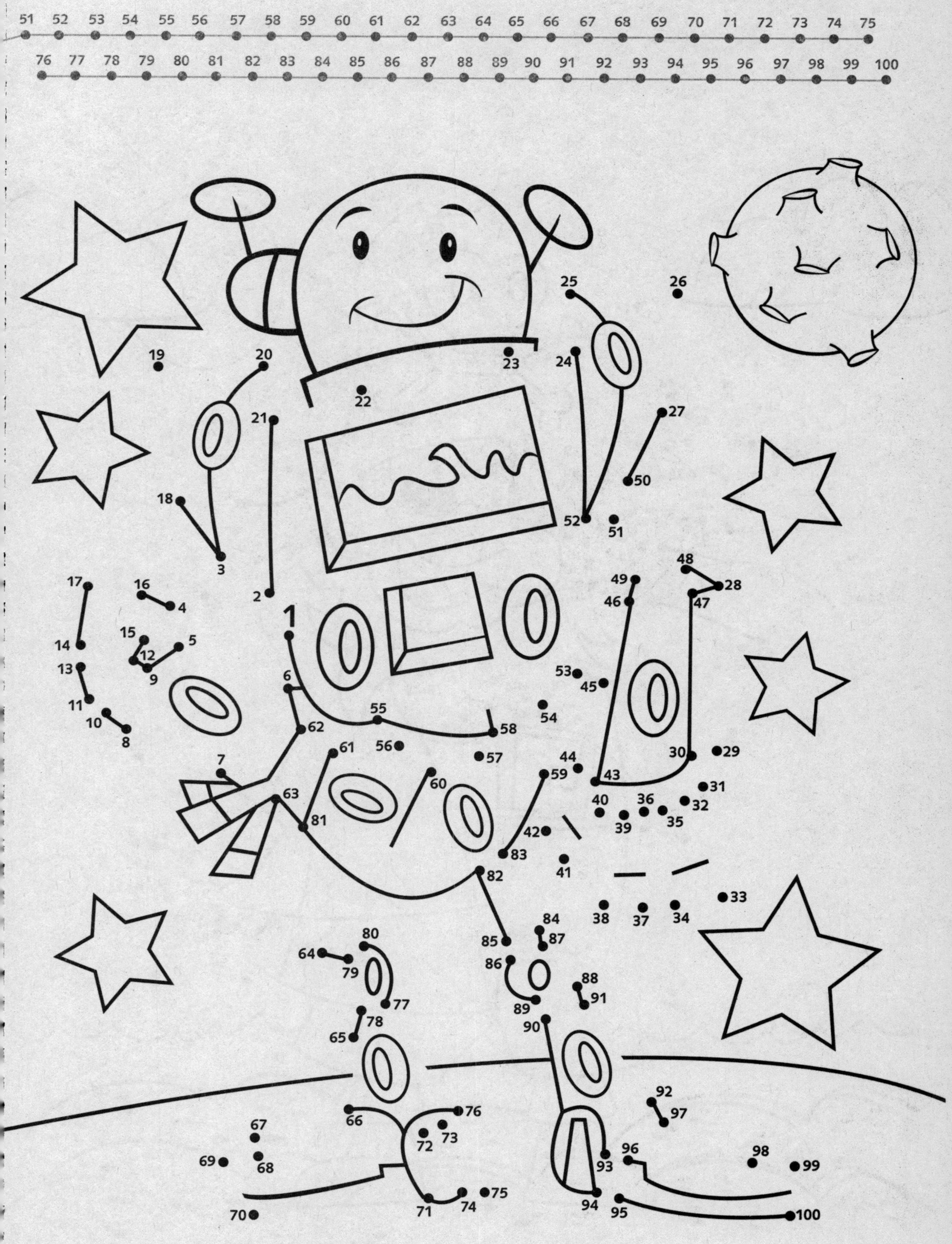

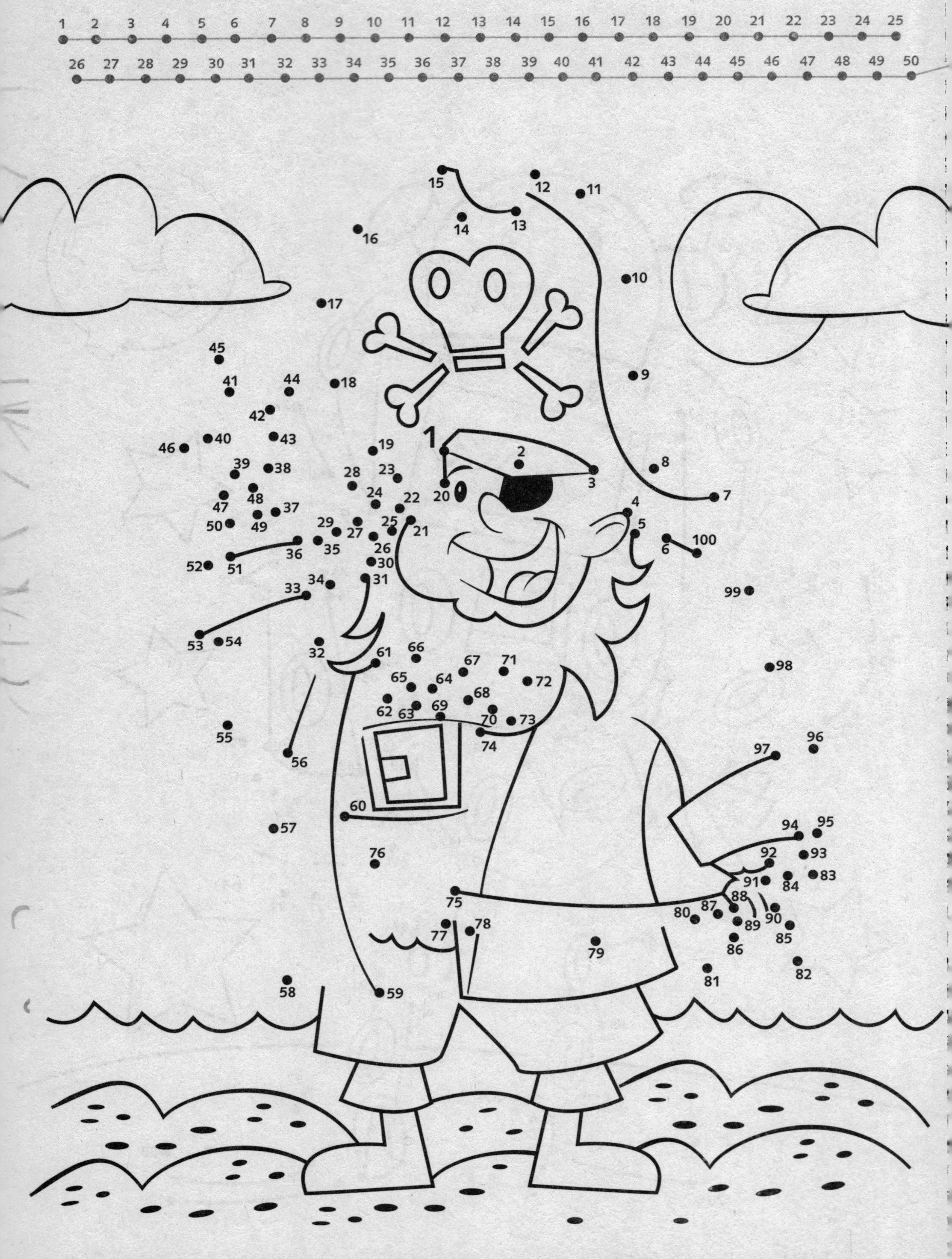

1 2 3 4 5 6 7 8 9 10 11 12 13 14 15 16 17 18 19 20 21 22 23 24 25

26 27 28 29 30 31 32 33 34 35 36 37 38 39 40 41 42 43 44 45 46 47 48 49 50

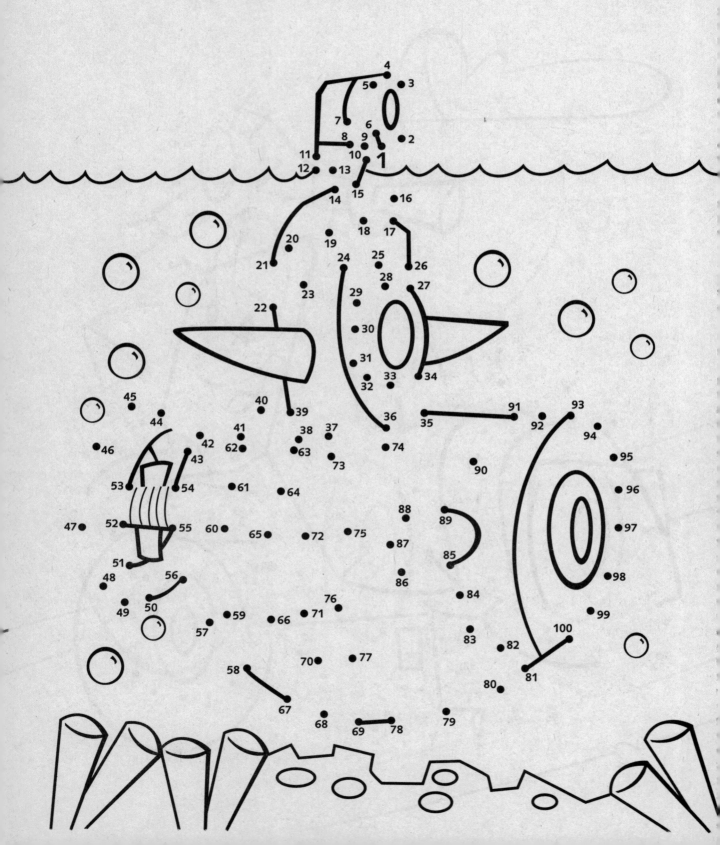

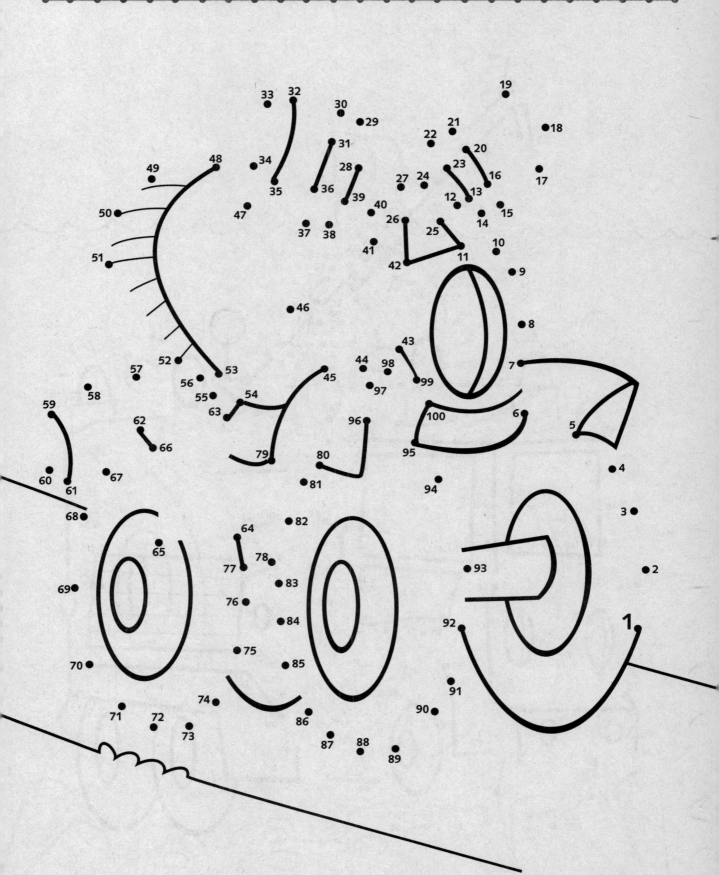

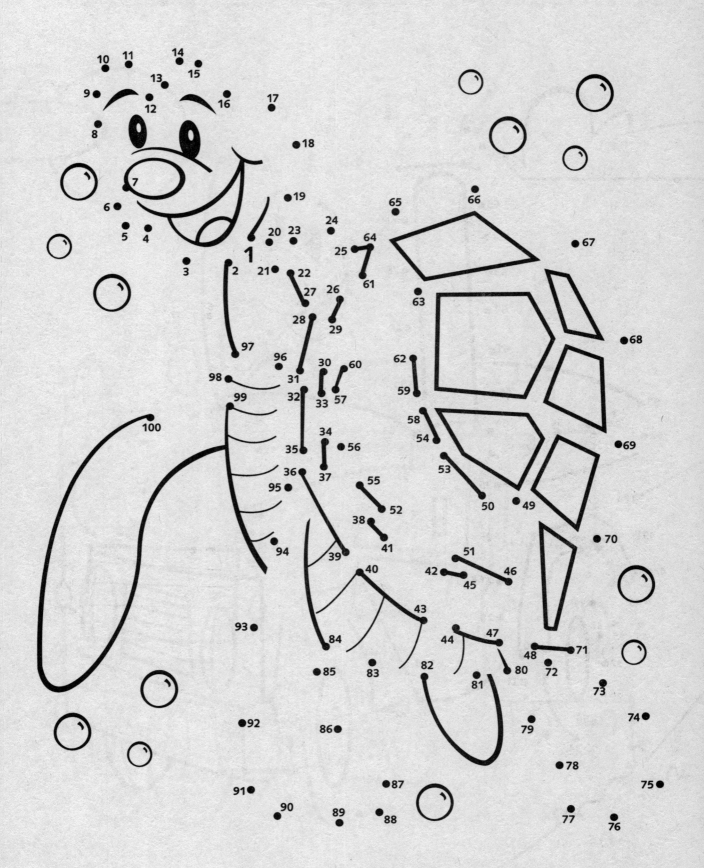

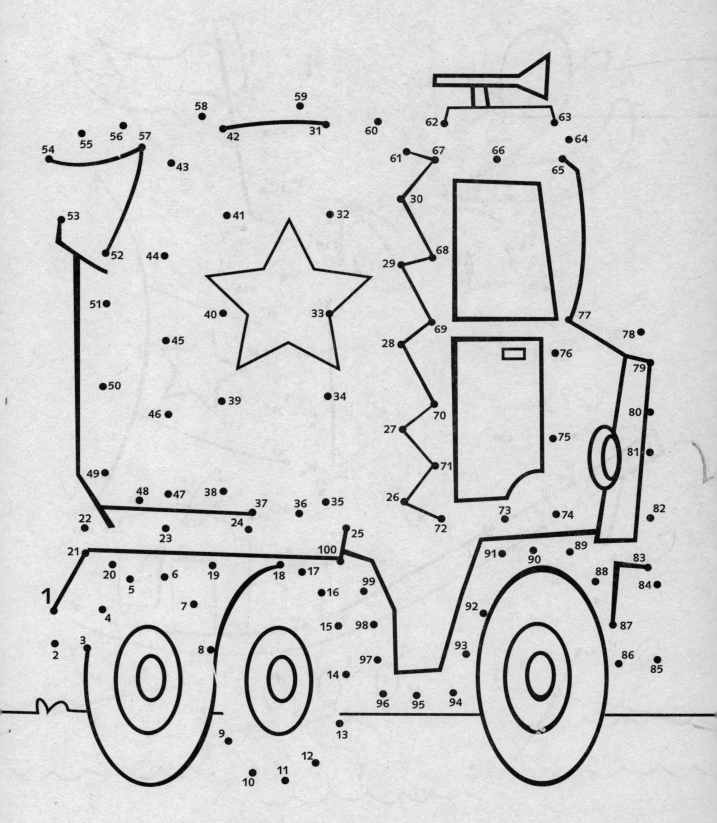

1 2 3 4 5 6 7 8 9 10 11 12 13 14 15 16 17 18 19 20 21 22 23 24 25

26 27 28 29 30 31 32 33 34 35 36 37 38 39 40 41 42 43 44 45 46 47 48 49 50

2

1

36

3

35

4

27

5

28

37

34

50

51

52

53

29

26

30

33

54

49

6

25

31

32

38

55

24

23

48

7

22

56

39

12

13

8

21

47

57

40

11

14

58

15

16

59

63

64

65

66

62

9

10

80

81

19

60

61

67

68

79

42

45

17

69

82

71

78

77

18

43

44

70

83

76

75

72

84

85

86

87

88

74

73

90

91

89

92

94

93

100

99

98

97

96

95

1 2 3 4 5 6 7 8 9 10 11 12 13 14 15 16 17 18 19 20 21 22 23 24 25

26 27 28 29 30 31 32 33 34 35 36 37 38 39 40 41 42 43 44 45 46 47 48 49 50

90

91

92

89

88 86 85 84 93 94 95

87 83 96

98 97

46 45

100 41 44

82 47 42 43

81 80

48 40

79

49 39

76 77

71 70 50 38

72 69 37

75 68 51 32

73 64 65 33

74 63 66 34

62 53 52 36 35 30

67 54 31

60 12 13 16 17 20 21 24 25 28 29

59 55 2

58 10 1

11 14 15 18 19 22 23 26 27 3

57 56 9 8 7 6 5 4

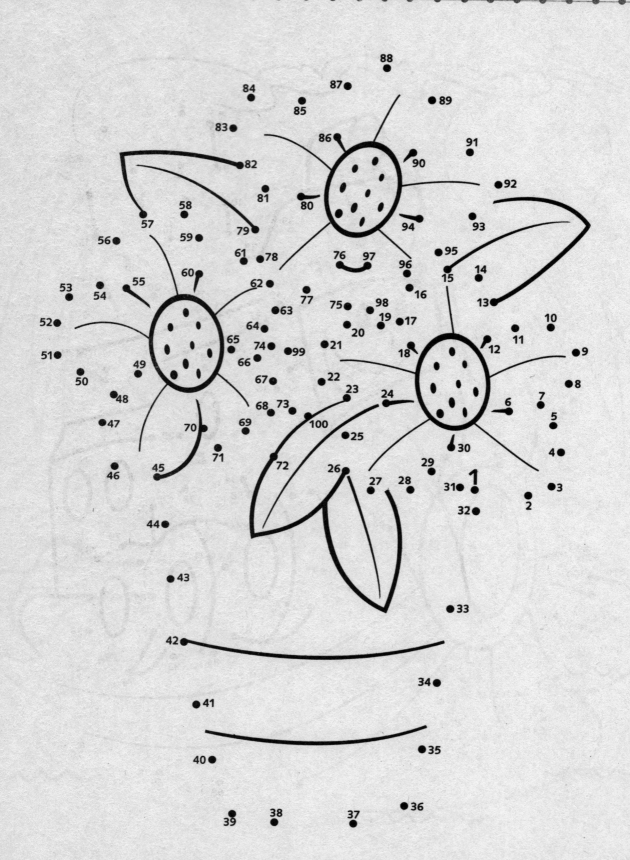

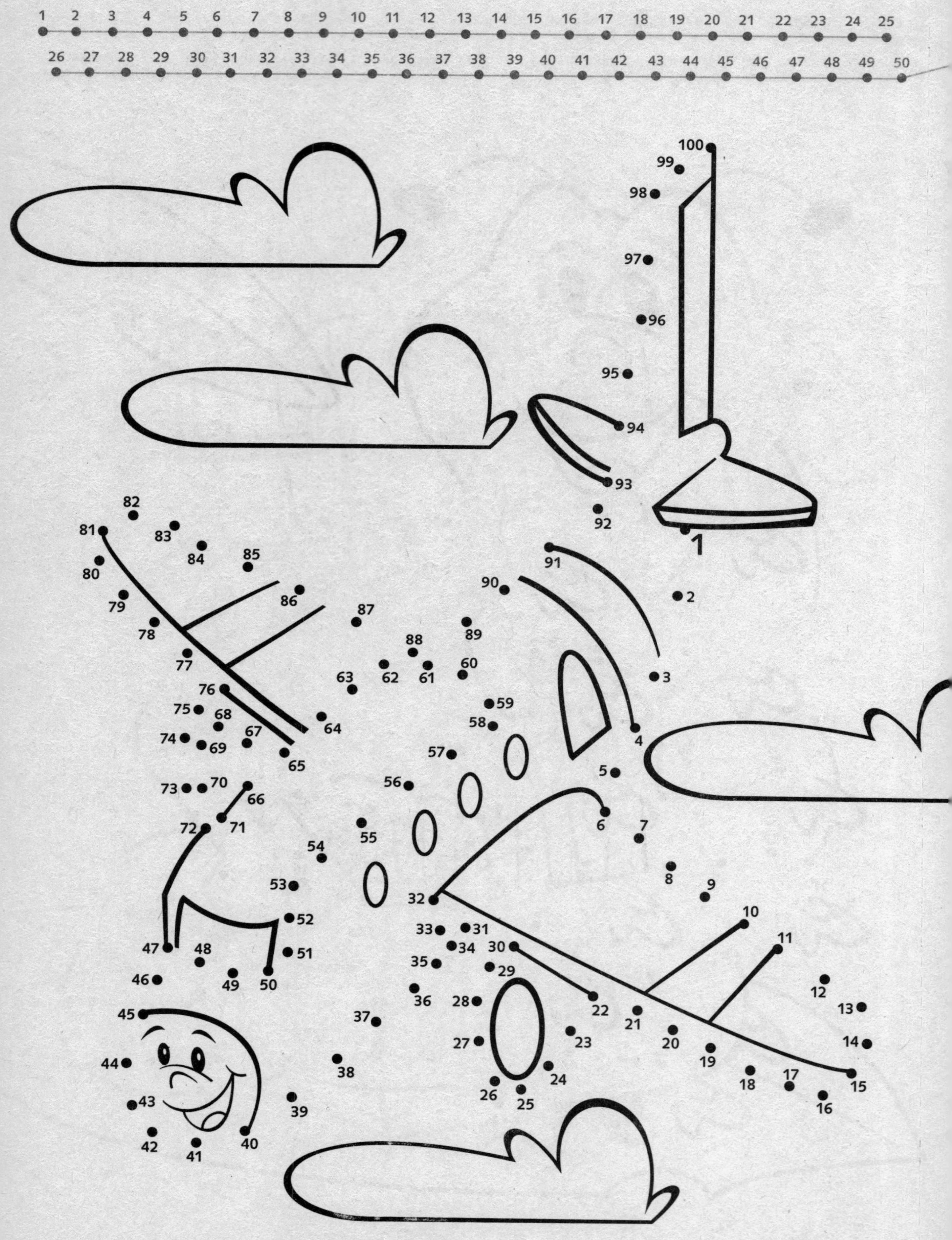
1 2 3 4 5 6 7 8 9 10 11 12 13 14 15 16 17 18 19 20 21 22 23 24 25
26 27 28 29 30 31 32 33 34 35 36 37 38 39 40 41 42 43 44 45 46 47 48 49 50

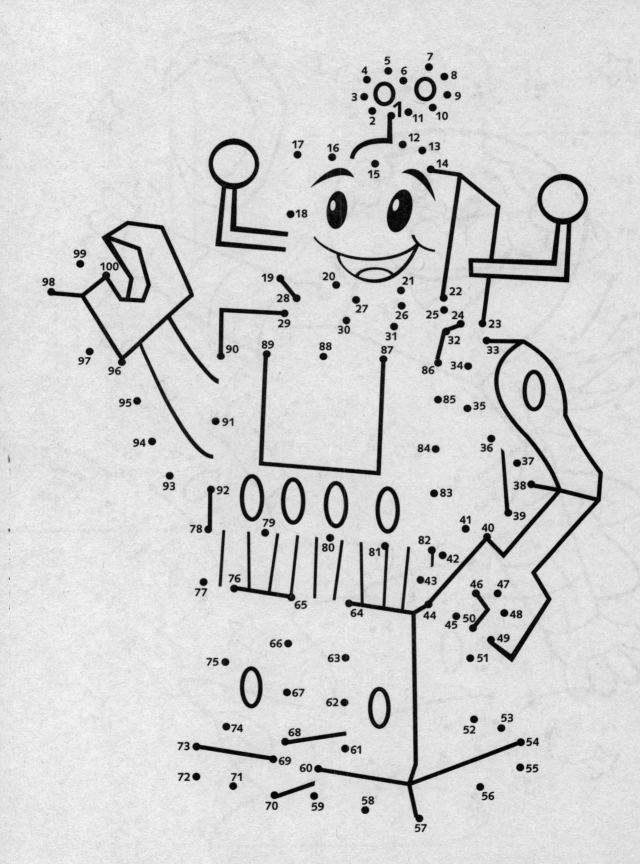

51 52 53 54 55 56 57 58 59 60 61 62 63 64 65 66 67 68 69 70 71 72 73 74 75

76 77 78 79 80 81 82 83 84 85 86 87 88 89 90 91 92 93 94 95 96 97 98 99 100

37

38
39
40

26
36
27
25
28 35
24
29 34
23
47 22
11
10 9
30 33
8
32
48 13
12 6
7 31
55 21
14
5
56
20
57 15
4
19
58 16
3
2
1
59 66 67
18 17
60 61 62 63 64 70
65 68 69 71
73 72
74
76 75

100 77

99 78

98 79

97 80
96 81
95 85 82
94 90
93 92 91 88 87 86 84
89 83

51 52 53 54 55 56 57 58 59 60 61 62 63 64 65 66 67 68 69 70 71 72 73 74 75
76 77 78 79 80 81 82 83 84 85 86 87 88 89 90 91 92 93 94 95 96 97 98 99 100